A DIRECTORY OF
QUEEN ANNE, EARLY GEORGIAN
AND CHIPPENDALE FURNITURE

ESTABLISHING THE PREEMINENCE OF
THE DUBLIN CRAFTSMEN

EARLY GEORGIAN DECORATED LACQUER CABINET ON GILDED GESSO STAND

Courtesy of Mallett & Son (Antiques) Ltd., London

A DIRECTORY OF

QUEEN ANNE, EARLY GEORGIAN AND CHIPPENDALE FURNITURE

ESTABLISHING THE PREEMINENCE OF THE DUBLIN CRAFTSMEN

F. LEWIS HINCKLEY

CROWN PUBLISHERS, INC., NEW YORK

PRINTED IN THE UNITED STATES OF AMERICA

PUBLISHED SIMULTANEOUSLY IN CANADA BY GENERAL PUBLISHING COM-PANY LIMITED

ABOUT THE AUTHOR

F. Lewis Hinckley is a furniture technologist, appraiser, and consultant. In a free-lance association with Parke-Bernet Galleries, Inc., New York City, he catalogued all of the European, British, and American furniture sold there between 1945 and 1951. He was the first to recognize the transmission of Irish designs, complete or in part, through craftsmen who settled in American cities such as Philadelphia and New York. He has traced this influence just as he has that of Continental artificers whose working styles have thus been apparent to him in the most elegant and sophisticated of Dublin examples.

As the first scientific study of British, and, in particular, Dublin, furniture, this publication is not offered as an exposé or criticism of the existing situation. It is the author's intention, rather, to popularize in its own right his particular choice as a collector himself of all the fine antique furniture he has handled professionally over the past forty years.

by F. Lewis Hinckley

A Directory of Queen Anne, Early Georgian and Chippendale Furniture
A Directory of Antique French Furniture
A Directory of Historic Cabinet Woods
A Directory of Antique Furniture

CONTENTS

A DIRECTORY OF
QUEEN ANNE, EARLY GEORGIAN
AND CHIPPENDALE FURNITURE

ESTABLISHING THE PREEMINENCE OF
THE DUBLIN CRAFTSMEN

ACKNOWLEDGMENTS

THIS STUDY CONCENTRATING ON THE ONE FIELD that over the years has become my favorite, could not have been completed without the helpfulness, encouragement, and contributions of good friends among dealers in antique furniture. Preliminary inquiries in this study were made to firms handling antique silverware, asking whether it was possible that such a high state of perfection in Irish silverware could have been attained without first obtaining a commensurable refinement in the furniture on which that silver was used and displayed. Further investigations were aided by the late Jack Treleaven (Needham's Antiques, Inc.), and Joel J. Wolff [J. J. Wolff (Antiques) Ltd.] recognized in this country generally as the most knowledgeable of professional authorities dealing in antique furniture.

My indebtedness to the late Karl Freund, who awoke my interest in Ireland's great master craftsmen with his explosive "What IMAGINATION those fellows had!" cannot be acknowledged too often. Relying upon scientific method rather than opinion, the outstanding examples Freund pointed out as representative of the finest Irish work took up to eight years to prove methodically, but these can now be recognized as originating in Dublin itself.

I owe a real debt of gratitude to the late Noel Hartnell, editor of the *Irish Tatler & Sketch*. In our exchange of photographs—mine of Irish and Dublin furniture, his of every print requested that illustrated his articles on old Irish castles and mansions and their furnishings—he was most generous indeed. John P. Ryan (Smith & Watson) turned over to me a fine collection of photographs and half-tone illustrations, which were invaluable in uncovering the Irish or Dublin origins of certain pieces I was tracing at that very time.

I am most grateful to every contributor who honored my requests for one or more photographs. English contributors to my book on cabinet woods have been even more generous with regard to the present subject. F. Roy Stamp (Biggs of Maidenhead Ltd.) has provided real encouragement and pleasure through the friendly comments in letters that accompanied photographs of the wonderful pieces he has handled, including some loaned from his private album. E. G. Williams, Mallett & Son (Antiques) Ltd., offered the help of L. M. Synge, who might possibly have done this work much more easily than I.

All of the museums, art galleries, and collections represented here have been prompt and generous in giving me access to their publicized exhibits. The Victoria and Albert Museum, in particular, has been especially helpful. It has supplied me with numerous, otherwise unavailable, examples.

Christopher Gilbert, keeper of Temple Newsam House in the city of Leeds, was so thoughtful when he supplied a requested photograph as to advise me that the piece shown was similar to one with an Irish provenance. In turning to him for information on a particular collector's magnificent architectural cabinet I had shown discernment beyond expectation. Through his help, that piece is available here as an invaluable illustration of a very limited number of Dublin "Vile and Cobb" cabinets of the utmost importance to museums and collectors.

From dealers not represented here I have received statements that it is impossible to distinguish Irish furniture from English furniture unless individual pieces can be traced back to original owners resident in Ireland. Without tracing or other proof, immediate acceptance as English must be the rule.* It would be strange indeed if Irish furniture could not be distinguished from that of England, despite the fact that furniture of every other country in the world may be so distinguished.

As a collector myself, I have come to know and value the relatively small coterie of firms represented here. In contrast to those firms who prefer to continue their misrepresentations of provenance, these firms have a broader, more ethical, attitude in terms of the fine pieces they handle and the clientele to which they cater. By their very inclusion in this study, which has already aroused some acrimonious protests, they have increased their stature and prestige. As a furniture technologist, appraiser, and consultant, I am certain that my own clients, as well as other similarly perceptive collectors, will agree here.

The integrity of these firms is in marked contrast with others who have wished to maintain the status quo, and wanted me to abandon this particular project. I have been informed that a typical Irish carved mahogany serpentine-front commode should not be called Irish since someone named "Jones" is said to have made a similar one, and his ancestors were said to have lived in London. Also, on the strength of one labeled London piece of the Regency period, all other somewhat similar pieces must be attributed to the maker whose name appears on that label, regardless of actual provenance.

Testimonies like this might well have deterred other investigations on this subject. They will no doubt be employed again by those whose collecting interests are not confined to authenticity, and who would rather disregard a provenance that is second to none for quality, design, interest, and, above all, *imagination,* in the entire history of antique furniture.

To all these friends of mine, I am sincerely grateful; to all friends of this particular study, it is sincerely and gratefully dedicated. Naturally my wife, Anne, is included in this dedication for her devoted interest in the book.

An additional interest in this research has been a concern that at long last recognition be accorded the honest and frequently brilliant furniture craftsmen who created the numerous masterpieces that arbitrarily have been credited to others of an entirely different nationality, having nothing whatsoever to do with their execution, or the particular genius that inspired the most successful of their delightful innovations. It is clearly evident in many of the superior Dublin examples that these great artificers found in that capital a haven from restrictions imposed upon them in their own countries, from which they sought to free themselves in the salutary atmosphere of a great and welcoming furniture center, larger and more active by far than any from whence they had come.

Collectors of American furniture will find that the illustrations here have been selected to show certain relationships between Irish and English furniture designs, and between Irish designs and those introduced and developed in America, sometimes by craftsmen who received their early training in Dublin, and occasionally both in Dublin and London. They may also serve in identifying the many pieces of Irish, or Dublin, furniture that appear in American

---

* It may not be amiss, as a footnote, to include my appreciation, also, of adverse criticism received months prior to the completion of this text and the arrangement of illustrations. These have included protests against the anticipated use of a provenance other than "English" in regard to *any* Irish (or Dublin) pieces formerly owned by those who complain about my study. Time is bound to prove the unprofitable nature of this attitude when the furniture shown here is finally recognized in its own right and is sought by collectors without uncertainty and restraint. Certainly, there is no intention here of drawing attention to either individual pieces or entire stocks owned by those opposed to the purpose of this study. Their protests have had real value, however, in suggesting the need for certain clarifications in the text and the inclusion of additional key illustrations that will result in a better understanding.

collections formed during the eighteenth century and later, such as the Chippendale settee formerly owned by Governor Wentworth (Ill. 323), which was confiscated and sold in 1776 by the federal government.

Only by chance or diligent research does one come upon recorded evidence of the long relationship existing between American ports and Ireland:

Philadelphia, 1739. Plunkett Fleeson, upholsterer, advertised his late arrival from Dublin, giving second importance to London in recommending his services.

Philadelphia, 1754. *To Ireland are sent . . . walnut boards.*

Alexandria, 1786. James McCormick advertised his *long experience in some of the first shops of England and Ireland.*

New York, 1798. Glass houses in Dublin working for the American trade had generally orders from New York *sufficient to occupy the factories for two years.*

Notices such as these might well inspire additional research into, and publication of, such pieces as mentioned above, as well as the multitude of Irish-American trade mirrors received here prior to the Victorian period. Compared to the relatively few Danish- and other Baltic-trade looking glasses, and a minimal number of those possibly traceable to English manufacture, by far the greater proportion of all our Queen Anne, Early Georgian, Chippendale, and later wall mirrors are accounted for only by our Irish-American trade, which was so extensive in this one respect as to warrant separate attention in a later directory.

AN INTRODUCTION TO
DUBLIN FURNITURE

MANY LEARNED PUBLICATIONS have been devoted to the subject of antique furniture produced in the leading capitals and major cities of Continental Europe and America. But not a word has appeared about the city which, with the possible exception of Paris, may well have been the largest furniture manufacturing center in all Europe: Dublin. For years, collectors have been able to recognize with certainty furniture originating in Paris, Venice, Stockholm, etc., or in Philadelphia, Newport, and even smaller towns in our own country. In contrast, a very large proportion—if not most of the finest, most interesting, and attractive examples—of antique furniture illustrated in the voluminous literature on old English furniture was not produced in England at all, and when accepted authorities have attempted to localize production in London, they are invariably mistaken. They recognize the furniture as capital-city work—but attribute it to the wrong capital.

This surprising lack of insight has allowed not only the public, but widely accepted experts on antique furniture to deny to Ireland any manufacture of furniture equal in quality and interest to the silverware, glass, and china, which lent but secondary decorative effects to the charming, stately, and magnificent city dwellings, country homes, and castles of Dublin, its environs, and the surrounding counties of its sovereignty.

In attributing British furniture on the basis of its exceptionally high quality to London origins, long-accepted English experts have disregarded any systematic consideration of designs, materials, structural techniques, marquetry patterns, hardware, ornamental mounts, and other details. Had they paid attention to these details, the repetition of basic forms with variations typical of any large furniture center would not have remained unnoticed. From close examination, it could have been determined that certain types of furniture were indeed the products of a single center, a large or capital city. With some study of related pieces shown *en situ* in published illustrations of Irish homes and their interior furnishings, or even of single, safely documented, pieces, whole groups of furniture of various kinds might have been traced to the proper capital.

Why then has the commercial and social importance of such a large, thriving city been so entirely overlooked by the generally perceptive public of our era? From contemporary reports we have been informed of the fine and even lavish furnishings of Irish homes. During the late eighteenth and early nineteenth centuries, the well-to-do Britisher divided his time between the London and Dublin seasons. During their stays in the Irish capital, visitors must have seen, priced, or acquired such furnishings. These acquisitions do in fact exist in numerous collections dating from that time throughout the British Isles, on the Continent, and in the Western Hemisphere.

How then could the entire furniture output of a major European capital become so generally unknown and unrecognized? The answer in part is a question of *popularity*. For centuries, Paris and London have been the two most popular cities with collectors influenced in their attitudes by the station, wealth, and material possessions of others. France and England have also been the most popular subjects in discussions of furnishings and objects of art. Thus, no doubt aided and abetted in some instances by the vanity or artfulness of our ancestors, facts of record have been altered or lost. As a result, it has been loosely accepted that furniture, in particular, has been received into various collections from either France or England. Thus, when one comes upon some of the most representative of Irish, or, more precisely, Dublin, pieces of furniture in Continental collections, one is told that they "came from England." The same is true of similar pieces appearing in American collections, some with attestations in attached, but meaningless, holograph labels. In Great Britain the confusion has reached a peak, bolstered on all sides by the names of royalty, personages of note, and great houses so formidable as to almost deter investigation or challenge.

It is reasonable to assume that in the normal course of trade, furniture produced in London was supplied to all the wealthier citizens in the city and to others in communities within reasonable delivery distance. This same reasoning applies to furniture manufactured in Dublin as well. However, such a comparison reveals that greater production was required in Dublin in supplying demands within her environs and elsewhere in the country since smaller Irish cities were so much larger than comparable English towns. In addition, home owners situated in English, Scottish, and Welsh areas closer to Dublin than to London are known to have ordered their best furniture directly from the Irish capital.

Thus, the greater amount of fine, identifiable Irish furniture surviving today can be accounted for by the large demands of wealthy Irish residents, absentee landlords, visitors during the Dublin social seasons, and the more affluent members of British communities located within easy shipping distance from the port of Dublin.

This study has disclosed various examples of Dublin furniture that are *recorded* as having been made for, or owned by, London notables of the seventeenth and eighteenth centuries. It is left to other researchers to produce more substantial proof that Dublin did in fact rival London within its own confines. As one incentive we suggest the wording of a genuine label, originally applied to a typical Dublin architectural pier mirror: "Kearney, Carver, Gilder & Looking Glass Maker to His Majesty." With the time lag often occurring in Irish designs, "His Majesty" would be George II *or* George III.

While little is known of the comparatively small amount of furniture produced in the secondary English towns, even less is known of furniture originating in Irish cities other than Dublin. These metropolises contained their own furniture manufacturers, and some employed famous furniture makers. Abraham Roentgen, for example, was employed in Galway after he was shipwrecked off Irish shores. But local innovations are likely to remain undefined unless evidence is now willingly offered in bills of sale such as the one enabling the identification of so many pieces made by William Moore of Dublin. At the turn of the last century, many such bills of sale must have remained in the hands of owners who preferred to protect their investments rather than reveal their true origin. If they are ever to be produced at this late date, such documents must come from individuals here referred to as *private sources of supply,* and they will no doubt remain uninterested in publicizing Ireland's national treasures as long as they repose in museums and collections of note.

Attention has been drawn to the work carried out in Dublin by the Italian Bossi, in supplying so many homes in that area with attractive, colorfully inlaid marble mantels, which in great numbers have now found their way elsewhere. Still no thought has been directed as to why he preferred carrying out his operations in Dublin rather than in London. Obviously, he must have been given an assurance of a better market. Also, it is generally known that

Angelica Kauffmann selected Dublin and its environs to pursue her career as a mural and portrait painter. She would hardly have made this move without the same assurance.

But these are minor questions. The most important inquiries that should have been made by former writers relate to the original sources of pieces acquired by dealers, and from whom they obtained photographs for publication. This information has been freely given by every English dealer represented here.

After stating that the amount of Irish furniture of fine quality that has survived from the walnut period "is so negligible that it demands no consideration from the collector," the leading English authority continued to illustrate piece after piece of such furniture despite his own advice. Had this author ever deigned to ask pertinent questions, many of these pieces could easily have been identified as having been acquired from Irish sources. By remaining unaware of such importations, he offered the more provincial of Irish work to the collector so that "He should, therefore, make himself familiar with the peculiarities of Irish design so that the recognition of examples will be easy."

A French authority has commented on the very small number of London furniture makers working over the same periods of time, in comparison to their known Parisian colleagues who were registered in guilds and carried on their operations under strict surveillance as to their qualifications and the merit of their work. Little is known of the relative standing of such English craftsmen who are listed only in London street directories. The work of very few is identifiable through safely ascertained original bills, inventories, and labels. More can be learned of possible London production through the offerings of designs published there. But these are not infallible guides either, since Chippendale's *Director* was followed, at least in some basic forms, in Dublin. In fact, Sheraton's designs were offered simultaneously in London and Dublin.

When London designers offered their followers side tables or consoles incorporating heavy animalistic forms, and satyr or other more or less human masks, it is only reasonable to assume that at least a sizable number of their offerings were actually produced. Nevertheless, very few have been safely identified. In contrast, a great number of similar pieces, long recognized as Irish side tables, have been scattered throughout the length and breadth of England since the beginning of the twentieth century, where they have been frequently illustrated in books and periodicals.

A similar preponderance of Irish over English furniture production is apparent in regard to tripod tables with tilting, rotating, or fixed tops of varying forms and with a wide range of edge treatments, as well as in Dublin-made elaborately formed, richly carved, handsomely inlaid, lacquered, or painted commodes carried out in Chippendale or Hepplewhite designs. This is also apparent in respect to French-Hepplewhite seat furniture with cabriole legs fashioned after the Continental popularity of transitional Louis XV and XVI forms, or the straight tapered, square, or round legs that followed. Indeed an inadequate acquaintance with the cabriole form is obvious in the puerile treatments it received in the hands of London draftsmen.

Irish taste for pleasing forms and ornamentation, even in utilitarian objects intended for ready and frequent use, is apparent in the number and variety of pieces of Dublin origin used for the service of wines, spirits, and tea. In this respect, the Dublin tray-top table and its elaboration into the so-called silver table is unique. Wine stands, cellarettes, tea caddies, tea trays, and teapoys received the same attention in shaping, carving, and inlaid decoration. Gaming tables allowed for equal or greater diversification. At the turn of the eighteenth century, the

Dublin taste for attractive ornamentation was also reflected in the embellishment of many forms of sofa and pedestal tables.

A wide acquaintance on the part of Dublin's master craftsmen with the materials in which they worked accounts for their selection and use of such exotic and valuable timbers as padauk, sabicu, maple knurlwood, bird's-eye maple, calamander, and zebrawood, as well as more readily obtainable woods such as yewwood, laburnum, and sycamore. All of the exotic timbers employed by *ébénistes* and *menuisiers* of Paris and other capitals of the Continent also came to Dublin or were easily obtainable directly across the Irish Sea at Liverpool. No doubt the large volume of trade with the Irish capital was partially responsible for the constantly increasing prosperity of that port.

Perhaps no better way of emphasizing the highly imaginative design and technical skills of the Dublin craftsmen is to contrast their work with that of their conservative, English colleagues. R. W. Symonds, the leading British authority, said: "The chief merit of English furniture is its simple and straightforward design. It is this characteristic which has undoubtedly given it so worldwide an appreciation. English furniture of the seventeenth and eighteenth centuries was made for a small population, and only a limited quantity is in existence."

Two decades ago an inquiry to the National Museum in Dublin brought the reply that "there are no criteria to distinguish what is Irish and what is English furniture." This very statement points out a deep lack of knowledge about English furniture itself! To this day it has been impossible for the accepted authorities to distinguish between work actually produced in London and work produced in the rest of England. This is certainly due to the fact that Irish furniture, especially furniture now readily identifiable as originating in Dublin, is represented as "English" in all of the literature on old English furniture.

Before beginning the task of providing the required criteria for tracing the development of fine Irish furniture, I attempted to determine the source of hundreds of examples that I could not accept as English by my own understanding of English conventions. Since I was quite unaware of the one principal source for these examples, I began my preliminary research in Holland, Germany, Denmark, and Sweden. It was interesting to discover certain parallel relationships, and the sources of some American trade mirrors, but I still had no inkling of how to carry out my research.

A first step in the right direction resulted from the inclusion of a handsome Irish staircase in a Long Island estate I had catalogued, one for which Karl Freund, a former antique dealer and decorator, supplied the furniture. In asking whether Irish furniture had accompanied the staircase, I received the explosive reply: "What IMAGINATION those fellows had!" With that one descriptive remark the picture started to unfold: *imagination* became a watchword in classifying Irish designs that have no equal among furniture masterpieces of the world.

One of the leading dealers in old English furniture around the turn of the nineteenth century and well into the early decades of the twentieth, Daniel Farr, maintained a stock of such quality and interest that he could command the highest prices in New York City. When I asked him if he had included Ireland in his buying trips, he explained that he had stopped going there around 1903, for by that time he was able to obtain the same high quality merchandise with less trouble by buying in London.

Popularity was also an important reason for declaring furniture English. Karl Freund explained, "Irish furniture was not popular . . . so we called it English." From the responses of less perceptive dealers, however, it appears that while they did recognize the more obvious Irish eccentricities, and possibly a few distinguishing provincialisms, they probably remained unaware of the skills developed in Dublin and therefore were led to believe that all furniture of superior quality represented in Irish collections could only have originated in England.

It might have been possible to counter these misleading opinions had some attention been paid to the scant but pertinent information and illustrations published by Percy Macquoid during the opening decades of this century, or if sufficient heed had been given to the histories and furnishings of Irish castles and mansions published over the years by *Country Life,* and more recently by the *Irish Tatler & Sketch.* Instead, the leading authority published the very finest of Dublin furniture and identified it as "English," or "London." In slashing out at those he considered rivals, he undertook to criticize Macquoid for not giving the "original sources" of the pieces he had illustrated. But he failed to realize that, by that time, such original sources had become the actual homes of English nobility or personages of note who were among the earliest collectors of the greatest Irish masterpieces.

We are, however, indebted to that authority for one valuable bit of information. After attempting to locate Irish records of furniture ordered or received from England, he remarked that "apart from Indian goods reexported from England . . . I have found no advertisements of imported furniture" *(Country Life,* March 14, 1952) . This may have had some effect on his too long postponed conclusion that—at least for others—if a piece of antique furniture "is known to have come from Ireland" it is presumed to "have been made there."

In stating that "Irish, or Anglo-Irish, craftsmen made on the spot the furniture the community needed," the same authority failed to recognize the working styles of those Continental artificers whose designs and techniques are so apparent in Dublin furniture development throughout the eighteenth century and early nineteenth.

While American and British dealers in old English furniture have unwittingly advertised or otherwise offered Irish furniture as English, duplicity is undeniable where Irish pieces have been obtained in Ireland and offered here as American, Philadelphia, or New York, or even as the work of known American craftsmen. It is quite understandable, however, from the very close approximation of some designs, how these pieces might unwittingly be accepted into other stocks or collections of American furniture, once they have passed through different hands. But this does not apply to the presence of Irish techniques, which differ from those followed in our own country.

In the case of tripod tables with piecrust-molded tops, Irish examples invariably differ in width and depth from treatments followed here, in which these edge moldings are wider and shallower. In tripod furniture, the dumbwaiter was not adopted here but, nevertheless, it has been recently accepted as an article of American production through a forced and thoroughly reprehensible authentification. A "Notable Collection of Beautiful English Furniture" was sold at the American Art Association in 1910. The catalogue* for the collection was prepared by the then leading authority on American furniture. Included in this collection was a typical Irish three-tier dumbwaiter that fetched $125. The same piece reappeared in 1954 at the sale of this same authority's estate, where it had been listed as a Philadelphia piece, and brought $3,100. Since then, other Irish dumbwaiters have also been offered as American.

---

* This catalogue of 404 illustrated lots, principally of Irish furniture, will be of considerable importance to any student of the subject fortunate enough to find a copy. It would also be revealing to those interested only in Early American furniture. My copy was studied, in 1951, by the late Jack Treleaven. His recognition at that time of Irish designs as produced in Philadelphia and New York was indeed surprising for such knowledge could hardly be expected of anyone specializing in old English furniture.

It has become the habit of a few dealers here to offer wing chairs or other upholstered furniture, purchased in the British Isles, as American on the basis of North American pine* or other common native woods, which are easily brought to the attention of the gullible through fall-away sections on their coverings. Since Irish furniture- and mirror-frame-makers were kept constantly supplied with these secondary materials through shipments from the United States and Canada, whenever the authenticity of such a piece is claimed by reference to these woods, the collector would do better in placing his reliance elsewhere.

The use of poplar, the particular and distinguishing choice of American cabinetmakers for secondary use, has also been employed in offering Irish furniture as American. The substitution of this wood, in the form of drawer bottoms or other parts obtained from comparatively valueless American pieces, to replace oak, pine, or other matching elements removed from some of the very finest Dublin cabinet pieces, may be carried out with relative ease and very considerable profit.

On the other hand, seat furniture may also be offered as American *despite* the appearance of another secondary wood—beech. The use of beech, which was introduced in Ireland in the sixteenth century, was apparently abandoned by joiners who arrived in Philadelphia, New York, and elsewhere in this country. Time and time again this abandonment has been proven by reports obtained through small samplings submitted to the United States Department of Agriculture, Forest Products Laboratory, Madison, Wisconsin. (It is now possible to distinguish between the European and American varieties of beech.)

Minor but effective changes in the appearance of Irish furniture have often been accomplished when more characteristic types of handles and escutcheons have been replaced by British brasses of simpler forms, either in old or new sets. When this form of deception is practiced in collections of American furniture, however, it may require the substitution of an old and very expensive set of typical American brasses. With such highly distinctive hardware, a Dublin cabinet that might otherwise have been described by English writers as made by the London firm of Vile and Cobb may be transformed into an exceptionally fine and costly American piece of museum quality.

Among the changes most easily carried out in meeting the demands of both the "old English" and "Early American" markets is that of elimination. Since Irish furniture occasionally departs from conventions generally associated with the more conservative styles of England and America, the removal of certain elements may be considered advisable. For instance, a cabinet or secretaire otherwise following the general lines of the Queen Anne or Early Georgian style will be surmounted by a fret-pierced pediment, indicating the retention of a basic form in a production of later date. Therefore, on the likely chance that the top surface will not be examined too closely, the identifying pediment is simply removed.† Another

---

* Supplies of American pine had been received in Ireland long before their appearance, around 1818, in England, where they "almost superseded the red and white pines, or Baltic Timber, which, up to that period, were the only kinds available for the purposes of the cabinet-maker." From this record it would seem that the appearance of American pine in British furniture or looking glasses dating before that time would be more likely to serve as evidence toward Irish, rather than English, manufacture. Since no record has been uncovered indicating an aggregation of Irish requirements, the one quoted above will at least indicate resources that could be brought to bear in meeting the demand for a preferred timber: The amount of pine timber annually imported to Britain from our North American colonies, on an average of eighteen years," beginning in 1823, is 9,634,776 cubic feet, employing upwards of three hundred vessels, the aggregate tonnage of which exceeds one hundred and sixty thousand tons." *The Cabinet-Maker's Assistant*, London, 1853.

† On the other hand, the addition or substitution of solid, cleft pediments to such cabinets or bookcases has resulted in increases of from 50 to 100 percent in their selling prices.

such piece may be surmounted by a typical Irish cartouche or similarly characteristic finials, any of which may easily be eliminated.

The deep tones of early mahogany imports were artificially approximated in some Irish work. By stripping such finishes to the bare wood and refinishing with clear shellac or varnish, the lighter tones generally associated with related Early American pieces are obtained. This process has been especially favored in cabinetwork. On one occasion a card table so treated might have been passed by in a general acceptance of an American stock had this not been just a few months after it had been examined and catalogued as English, with the usual reservation —probably Irish.

When certain elements have been too incongruous for acceptance as being of English design, more drastic alterations have been carried out. One such instance occurred in a piece owned by a lady who had built up a very prosperous business through her social connections in Ireland. This was advertised as a "Queen Anne side table with original grey marble top," although the illustration showed that the top had been replaced by a pine core surfaced with walnut veneer. The four cabriole legs displayed typical Irish leaf- and pearl-chain carving on the knees. When the piece came up at auction some years later, it was easily seen that the entire lower portion of the legs had been removed. Since there was no indication of the necessity to remove that portion of the legs, as when the lower parts of chair or table legs have become completely reticulated with worm channels, leaving only outer surface shells that may give way at any time, it can only be deduced that the legs originally terminated in one of the overelaborated types of "Spanish" paw or web feet that characterize the less attractive Irish treatments. These feet, however, had been replaced by simple club feet to achieve an earlier, Queen Anne effect. This piece was then handsome enough to be bought and delivered to the scion of one of the oldest and largest houses in the antique furniture business.

The otherwise universal method of classifying antique furniture seems not to have been understandable to certain British authorities. Thus, R. W. Symonds was led to complain that it was too bad "English" furniture could not be traced to an individual or shop with the ease with which Americans do this in regard to the "work of Duncan Phyfe" (!). This is inconceivable to bona fide Continental and American authorities and no doubt results from Symonds's inability to overcome confusion resulting from an acceptance of so much Irish furniture as English.

What the Americans have done in identifying the work of various states, towns, and individual craftsmen is comparable to what the French, Italians, Swedes, and others have done by comparative studies that have resulted in determinative classifications. British authorities can accomplish the same results only after they recognize that much of what they consider English is actually Irish or Dublin furniture. When this is understood, it may at last also be possible to distinguish between the work of London and the still loosely designated work of England as a whole.

Comparison is also employed in all other fields of the fine and applied arts for the classification of antique furniture. If an unsigned painting is believed to represent the work of a known artist, or a bronze statuette that of a known sculptor, the only way a determination may be made is by *comparison,* and correct decisions in these fields may be more difficult to arrive at than in regard to antique furniture.

For example, I was able to prove to the satisfaction of an auction official that a commode catalogued as French provincial was not only Swedish, but made in Stockholm. By comparison with his other work, I was able to attribute the commode to a particular, if little known, cabinetmaker. In connection with Irish furniture, it is indeed unfortunate that, at present, only the work of William Moore is widely known—and that through a preserved bill. By his now recognized marquetry patterns, some, if by no means all, of his executed designs have been identified. If bills of other Dublin craftsmen come to light, their work will be similarly traced, though it is to be hoped in a less halfhearted way than Moore's. In a single museum collection, a Moore piece is properly labeled as his, while his other pieces are still loosely classified as English, though, of course, not London, since there is no known London furniture that bears a comparative likeness.

An example more pertinent to this particular study concerns a mahogany commode, one that was so baroque in design and carving as to prompt R. W. Symonds to drop his speculations on the work of various unknown European schools in favor of a supposedly all-covering "Continental." It was tentatively designated as "North German" when I was asked to look at it. English authorities have paid little attention to the fact that cabinet hardware can be of great importance. The elaborately wrought handles of this piece also appear on another of these commodes illustrated by Percy Macquoid, which I had already proved as Irish. On the basis of these handles and a meaningless note on the work of Juste-Aurele Meissonier, this "wild" Irish piece was sold as English at a price of $6,500.

Professionals with varying degrees of awareness of the present state of Irish furniture, and even a nonprofessional authority like R. W. Symonds, have agreed that if a particular piece of antique furniture is known to have come from Ireland it may be accepted as originating there. Thus, if I describe a rather plainly fashioned piece such as a writing table, a pedestal desk, or a chest of drawers as Irish and as being distinguishable from English furniture through certain minute details and original hardware, this is not an accurate statement. For while there have been, and still are, such pieces in Irish collections—and they may correctly be accepted as Irish when they appear in illustrations of such collections—there is no basis as yet on which one may say that they approximate or differ from English examples. If such pieces appear in English collections, of either long or short standing, *they may not* be considered as originating there since, as a whole, such collections have been added to or entirely formed during the worldwide transportation of fine Irish furniture, which began around 1875 or earlier and continues to this day. For accuracy, therefore, one must say that such plainly fashioned pieces are distinguishable not *from* English pieces but *as* Irish, or Dublin, because of certain determining details: structural features, moldings, ornamentations, etc., *in combination with original and distinctive hardware*. If the more important criteria are eventually forthcoming in respect to English furniture, we may *then* be able to distinguish *between* furniture of the two countries in general.

The trifling amount of attention paid to Irish furniture has only hindered its study as a whole since, aside from a very few illustrations published by Percy Macquoid, it has generally been described as provincial, incongruous, or otherwise lacking in refinement. Illustrations of fine Irish productions, and any others likely to be of such provenance, which have appeared in books and magazines which, from 1903 on, have been devoted to old English furniture, were removed and combined with many hundreds of photographs to form my files for this one particular class of antique furniture. These illustrations were arranged in orderly sequence showing the regular development of designs according to each category of furniture in each style period. They have been constantly added to, mainly through the documentary pieces advertised by leading dealers, which often provide the principal interest and value in collectors' magazines.

As this scientific method of classifying Irish furniture progressed from a mere handful of documentary examples to dozens, then hundreds and, over the years, to thousands, it became increasingly rewarding to obtain confirmations in one category through proofs arrived at in another. Thus, a Dublin card table (Ill. 181) would be independently proven in one category, and a similarly classified chair would be found to have been made to match, through similar details of design including the same apron-shaping. In classifying a series of Chippendale commodes, it would be found that one of the pieces (Ill. 423) coincided with the lower central unit of a bookcase, which appeared in a sequence of larger Dublin cabinet pieces arrived at independently. For a single example of the minor but surprising confirmations that occur periodically, the "Gothic Writing Table" illustrated in *Georgian Cabinet-Makers,* 1955, Fig. 103 (above the Dublin chest of drawers from Badminton House), and determined as a Dublin piece, was noticed to have its lateral doors faced with blind-fret ornamentation approximating that of the central interior desk section of a long proved Dublin secretaire (Ill. 440).

This systematic comparative method gradually developed into what may be termed the first scientific study of antique furniture produced within the British Isles, which, in providing the *criteria to distinguish what is Irish* furniture, may also eventually provide a determination of *what is English furniture.*

By including every possible detail of Irish, or Dublin, pieces and others in which such proof is sought, the files approached the efficiency of a modern computerized* system. In this respect, general designs, basic forms, and common elements continue to be of first importance, but additional evidence is readily available in carved or inlaid ornamentation—moldings, bandings, and borders; variations in the interior fittings of bureaus and secretaires; turnings, fret patterns, finials, and other crestings; hardware, such as handles, escutcheons, lever-lock discs, hinges, grilles, ornamental mounts, toe caps, sabots, and so on.

These exterior features, which are so easily seen and compared, are more important than those requiring interior examination. Construction has been an overrated topic with writers who have undertaken the subject by describing as typical of English construction the Irish pieces they have shown in photographic illustrations and detail drawings. Some structural methods and/or preferences in secondary materials have value in relation to Continental and American furniture, but, Irish methods of construction were based on Continental as well as British styles, or were more or less successful improvisations.

Through this standard system of comparison, combined with working studies, it has become apparent that Irish furniture, even that of Dublin, often is two or more decades later than the circa dates generally associated with various designs; in some instances, the difference may be two or more style periods. By casual observation, such pieces will therefore appear to have been produced during the William and Mary, Queen Anne, and Early Georgian periods. Their actual dates of execution, however, must be determined by technical and ornamental methods or by details that were not introduced or developed in that country or city until long after such styles and designs are supposed to have passed out of vogue.

In this particular respect some astonishment is apt to result from the examples introduced here of so-called Charles II or William III decorated lacquer cabinets on elaborately carved

---

* The term computerized system may not find favor with some, in particular those best able to recognize the accuracy of its findings through their own firsthand knowledge of Irish furniture as obtained directly through private sources in that country. For accuracy and clarity, Webster's *New Twentieth Century Dictionary,* 1966, cites: "Computerize —2. To operate, *produce, control, etc.* by or *as if by means of* electronic computers." [italics mine]

and pierced stands, "circa 1675" or "circa 1700," which were actually produced long after: *two or more style periods later,* during the middle decades of the eighteenth century. Indications of this late manufacture have been all too obvious. Rarely, an otherwise typical mahogany paw-foot side table has appeared with Charles II carved and pierced foliage festoons depending from the frieze and supporting balanced figures of cherubs. Still, such evidence, and the knowledge obtained through a study of the decorations applied to these cabinets, has gone unnoticed by the accepted authorities.

British antique dealers now frequently abandon the use of these often meaningless circa dates in favor of designations according to design and origins within the eighteenth century or early nineteenth. This is certainly a wise procedure. It reflects sound judgment and eliminates a practice which, while possibly imparting a certain scholarly *éclat,* has too often resulted in errors of judgment.

It would seem impossible that evidence of provenance of a piece of furniture could ever be found in a large, clearly lettered notice on the piece itself. Yet this has happened, although it has been ignored by everyone from the first publication of *The Present State of Old English Furniture* to the new and revised edition of the *Dictionary of English Furniture.* Both of these works illustrate a small desk; its slant lid prominently inlaid with the legend: "A TREE 8 Yards about and Fifty high 100 pound value when blown down by ye great wind 1703 in *Stratton Park.*"

The British and Irish Railways office, when still located in New York City, informed me ·that they knew of no such park in London; and from the large number of related desks, card tables, and cabinets on stands, it was obvious that these could not have been produced in any of the smaller towns of England. "Was there a Stratton Park in or near Dublin?" "Of course, Stratton Park was one of Ireland's great playing fields." "As far back as 1703?" "As far back as the seventeenth century, at the very least!"

In their failure to accept the information so painstakingly offered in this permanently fixed message, the authors and revisers of these publications have just as clearly shown a lack of purpose totally alien to the serious nature of true research. It would appear that only the words "Made in Ireland" stamped on the piece would arrest their attention.

The Present State of Old English Furniture also features an important marquetry cabinet-on-stand with spiral-turned supports; its stretcher has helped to prove the origin of many Dublin desks, card tables, and cabinet pieces. Shown in this book with a circa date of 1675 (two or more decades, or two or more style periods later), the same authority later presented that cabinet as "Flemish." This merely revealed a profound lack of knowledge of a second field of antique furniture.

In examining a Chippendale drop-leaf table on exhibition prior to the auction in which it was to be sold, I noticed beneath the drawer bottom a London label which, if it was original, would have disproved a large number of related pieces I had already classified as Irish. Fortunately, this too proved to be another instance of abuse of labels. On close inspection, the label was found to be false, and it was agreed by the auction authorities that its presence was better left unmentioned.

Among several published examples of labeled furniture attributed to an English cabinet-maker, the most incongruous to me in its design and decorative treatment is the attractive, fanciful secretaire that has been claimed to be the work of one Hugh Granger, who apparently died in 1706, four years prior to the circa date given for this production. (Edwards and Jourdain, *Georgian Cabinet-Makers,* 1955, Figs. 210, 211.) To me, this piece is entirely characteristic of the delicate and graceful interpretations of the more inspired Dublin artificers. The desk section, in the up-scrolled shaping of its vertical drawer partitions, coved drawer fronts, and center arched recess flanked by pilasters, including the exact arrangement of all these identifying features, is precisely duplicated in the popular Dublin bureau-form dessing mirrors. This slant-front section is also similarly treated in other secretaires on straight or cabriole supports, here identified as specialties of Dublin artificers rather than their more practical and substantially inclined London colleagues. Of particular identifying importance is the manner in which the lacquer decoration has been carried out. There is the characteristic use of willows overhanging a porch raised on pilings in rippling water; birds zoom with outspread curving tail feathers around an urn of flowers. This and the balance is typical of the best Dublin artists in this medium. The actual date of this piece will coincide with the use of mahogany in the manufacture of J. Roy Stamp's interesting Early Georgian tray table (Ill. 168), featuring the identical squared cabriole legs with modified scroll feet. With the number of narrow bureaus-on-stands now known to have originated in Dublin rather than London, this label on a solitary example cannot be convincing and warrants further investigation.

With pieces sent for sale at auction, it has been the custom simply to ignore dishonestly applied labels. It is the understanding in this country at least that auction executives assigned to catalogue antique furniture are expertly informed as to values only, while writers on the subject are generally considered to be experts on genuineness or antiquity. Therefore, with the appearance of a piece that has been published as bearing the label of a maker, the consignor can expect and demand that such a piece be presented in the auction catalogue just as it was represented when acquired, or just as it has been published. Hence, collectors seeking to acquire any piece of unusual importance that has been published should seek advice from the more knowledgeable professional dealers, a practice that auction officials will cheerfully recommend.

The simple fact that the Duke of Beaufort was a subscriber to Chippendale's book has been accepted by the authorities mentioned above as evidence that furniture "of conspicuously high quality" and "very original" was delivered to him from Chippendale's premises in St. Martin's Lane, London. This may be standard evidence in the field of old English furniture, but it is not research. It points out, again, a general blindness about where the furnishings of Badminton House originated, not only those in the Chippendale taste but the walnut-marquetry and decorated-lacquer pieces illustrated by Percy Macquoid during the opening decades of this century.

As Dublin is not directly across from Gloucestershire, the shipping distance from London to Badminton would be only about twice that from Dublin. But why should the Duke have turned away from an old proven source which, with its special skills in fretwork, metalwork, lacquer, and so on, was so well equipped to meet his taste in furniture for a Chinese bedroom? In fact, if all the Badminton House furniture in the Chinese taste is taken into consideration, the Duke's ideas present no problem at all. The pieces he chose would hardly have warranted the additional cost if indeed his taste could have been as well suited in London.

The attempt to achieve accurate, scientific results has prompted me to seek rejections or confirmations of my findings from a specialist in Far Eastern art, and a firm specializing in Early American furniture. I sent a photograph of a lacquer cabinet-on-stand selected for this book by L. M. Synge to another friend, Frank Caro, whose knowledge of Chinese lacquer is second to none. I explained that this was an important example of those "Indian cabinets" brought from China and elsewhere in the East by ships of the British East India Company, that these stands were also made to support cabinets copied from such imports, and asked for a date and, if possible, a more definite provenance. His reply was that this particular cabinet (Ill. 226) had been made in Shanghai or the south of China during the latter half of the eighteenth century. Following this, I sent Frank Caro a group of twenty-one photographs and halftone illustrations of Oriental cabinets with varying types of stands. Except for a single example, which he dated late seventeenth century to early eighteenth, the majority of these published examples were dated late eighteenth century, two had been made from screen panels, and one was Korean. My conviction regarding these cabinets, both Occidental and Oriental, and their stands was once again confirmed.

My second letter was prompted when two fret units that occur with some frequency in Dublin work were found to appear in exactly the same conjunctive use on the legs of a Chippendale open-arm easy chair said to have been made by Thomas Affleck of Philadelphia (Ill. 329). Another characteristic—a leaf carving extending the full length of the serpentine arm supports—was decidedly more typical of Dublin than of Philadelphia work. Before reaching a final conclusion, my only photograph of this chair was sent for examination to a firm specializing in American furniture, with a letter asking whether Thomas Affleck ever worked in Dublin or elsewhere in Ireland. Only if this had happened could all of the characteristic Irish details have appeared, together, in an American-made piece.

Weeks later a letter from that firm contained the following concluding sentence: "You asked about your chair, and some fret elements—please explain." This could mean that only the inquiry had been received, but not the photograph. An immediate long distance call was met with the reply that nothing was known of a photograph of a chair being received from me! With my own insistence that the photograph had been carefully mailed, must have been received, and would be traced by the postal authorities, it was finally admitted that it had been received, that the sale in which the chair had come up was known, as was the name of its buyer.

Evidence of this kind is far more positive than any written opinion, and in this case more than conclusive. Had the photograph shown a genuine American chair there would have been no concern over its publication as Irish, Portuguese, or Chinese! This would have been shrugged off as the work of an uninformed amateur. However, publication of this Dublin chair with its true provenance (the source of so many other "Philadelphia" chairs, stools, and settees, and other Irish or Dublin productions included in, or added to, collections of American furniture formed during the eighteenth, nineteenth, and twentieth centuries) had been regarded, quite obviously, in a different light, outweighing any consideration of moral conduct.

As it has become possible for a representative picture of Irish furniture to unfold, it has also been evident that certain prominent names appear frequently as inheritors of early collections of Irish, and especially Dublin, pieces. This has made it quite apparent that a number of these inherited pieces were made in Dublin expressly for the forebears of the present or late owners.

In addition to the many collections open to Percy Macquoid for illustrating the first monumental presentation of British furniture, those later formed by Lord Leverhulme and Percival Griffiths have been drawn upon in adding to that coverage. Both of these collections were composed largely of fine Irish pieces, which, at the time of their formation, were flooding the English market and overflowing in all directions. The Leverhulme collection was thus dispersed in New York City. Access to the Griffiths collection accounts for R. W. Symonds' excellent taste in the most important examples of Dublin furniture. He identified these in books and articles mainly as English, but occasionally as very superior "London" work: "by a German craftsman resident in London," as "Flemish," as "Continental," and so on. He would brook no dissent in his descriptions of favorite examples, even when he described Dublin pieces of superb quality: "Dutch or German inlay," marquetry with "French or Flemish influence," "the best London-made drawers," "mounts made in England," "strongly Continental in design." He would ask and then answer his readers: "In what country was this commode made?" "There can be only one answer: It was made in England by one of the numerous German or French cabinetmakers who emigrated there." A wealth of excellent illustrations of Dublin examples serves to refute these theories.

Findings presented here as a result of the systematic method of classification that has been followed are not theories or opinions. These opinions were found wanting in the captions of my first publication although, with the help of trusted friends in the trade, they represented the best knowledge then available in regard to both English and Irish furniture. Native examples of outstanding quality, in designs appearing with some frequency or with normal variations, are logically specified as originating in Dublin. Other examples through their appearance in this study are shown as Irish, although that does not preclude eventual assignment to Dublin. Because of limited documentation as to dates associated with certain designs, circa dates will be used sparingly, although all pieces are shown as antique.

Some pieces of British furniture, largely through their virtuosity, are quite obviously of Dublin origin. As they are so highly individualistic in their design, it is impossible to prove them in the usual way, for no comparable examples exist, at least as far as these extensive files are concerned. It may be years, if ever, before any such examples do appear. Still, of these individual creations a few seem too important to withhold from future studies of British furniture. Therefore, the term "British" will be used in such instances to indicate that, in my *opinion,* such pieces do not come within my understanding of London traditions in this field, but are more representative of the unusual, imaginative, and highly creative effects in Dublin work. Lesser English towns do not enter into such consideration for I have never seen any considerable departure from the usual conservative English traditions in the very limited number of pieces known to have been made in these places. Such a thriving English furniture center as Lancaster, which has received much attention from writers on old English furniture because of the presence of the Gillows factory there, had at its peak a population of only 9,030.

Values of the finest, most sought after, examples of Dublin furniture will remain the same regardless of whether they are properly designated or continue to be so loosely and irrationally assigned to England. As auction prices have shown, collectors will always appreciate these pieces for their quality, interest, and decorative value regardless of either professional or amateur assignments. Should ever a decision rest on whether such a piece was made in Dublin, or possibly somewhere among these lesser English towns and hamlets, a determining pecuniary value must rest with a capital-city provenance.

If all the advertisements published between 1903 and the present of only the very finest Dublin furniture could be reproduced in a series of volumes devoted to the major developments of each style period, the resulting effect on public taste and approval would be instant and far-reaching. This single volume can serve only in a very limited introductory capacity, showing only a small number of such pieces. If this study can assure a better understanding and increased appreciation of other examples, similar to or approaching those that have been made available here photographically, the principal object of these researches will have been accomplished. Dublin furniture will then be sought after for itself by the same otherwise discerning collectors who have heretofore acquired it as "English," and Irish designs will be acknowledged when reproduced, not only by firms such as Hicks of Dublin, and Smith and Watson of New York, but by all other leading British and American furniture manufacturers.

The one indisputable means of assessing the value of any particular class of antique furniture is by the prices individual pieces have commanded over the years. There has been a rise and fall of interest in various fields during the past hundred years. At the same time, Irish furniture in general, and the finest Dublin examples in particular, has continued to increase in price. To emphasize this popularity, I have included the prices that some of these pieces have brought at auction sales in New York City and London. It should be understood, however, that such figures seldom indicate retail values, which must be based upon many factors with which the auction house is not burdened.

Since I have found it wise, and indeed necessary, to depart from convention by removing illustrations from books on old English furniture and retaining them in my files (often without indicating their sources with the patience and exactitude of a proper librarian), I am faced with two alternatives. Either I share with the more serious students of design some important documentary illustrations through greatly abridged references to authors and their various books and editions, or I disregard this additional documentation, which has taken years of *my* time to locate and prove. I understand that parallel studies may be in progress, so it would seem selfish to follow the easier course. Therefore, these shortened references will be included here.

CORROBORATIVE EVIDENCE

IT IS PRESENTLY IMPOSSIBLE TO DETERMINE dates of execution with any exactness for the earliest examples of Irish metropolitan designs. Judging from the designs developed in Holland, Germany, Denmark, and Italy, some speculation is possible upon their transference, in part or in whole, to Ireland. But Continental authorities are not as interested as English writers in claiming early dates. Any such research must of course take into consideration the latest, rather than the earliest, distinguishing features of designs developed in a country through the talents of its native craftsmen and those of its adopted colleagues.

No doubt a better acquaintance with internal affairs—the undiscovered reasons for Dublin's considerable increase in population during the second decade of the eighteenth century, and just how much this owed to possible foreign immigration—would have been helpful in this study. Continental authorities, concerned enough to discuss hundreds of Dublin designs that were unrecognized at the time, easily recognized various techniques fostered in their own capitals. The earliest of these invariably dated from the second or third decades of the eighteenth century. Their observations are borne out in regard to London furniture by the large set of dining chairs of pure Dutch design (*Georgian Cabinet-Makers*, Pl. 10) ordered from Richard Robert for Hampton Court, their "William and Mary" design "invariably dated about 1700" by English authorities, but the warrant for their production dated "October 21, 1717."

How then, with a time lapse so general in the transmission of these earlier designs as rendered in the British capital, can such pieces relate to the improbable dates also *invariably* assigned to them by the same authorities? The only safe attribution in this respect would be *early eighteenth century*, for pieces determined as having been made prior to 1750. That is the form recognized here, with the use of *Queen Anne* only insofar as this term has served in its long acceptance as a more or less recognized style, and with *Early Georgian* similarly indicative only of pre-Chippendale designs—which designs, in some instances continued to be developed long after publication of Chippendale's *Director*, just as Chippendale designs remained in some favor throughout and after the turn of the century.

Irish chairs and settees incorporating an especially favored treatment of arm, leg, splat, and so on (or a portion of such an element, such as a foot) were frequently developed in different designs. Often this makes it impossible to maintain or display a sequence of designs based on such individual elements. For instance, the Dublin shepherd's-crook arm appears as a feature of some early walnut seat furniture and in later Georgian mahogany examples, and then deteriorates into a modified crook and finally into a simple continuous bent arm. One such peculiarity—possibly resulting from a combination of native and foreign preferences—is the use of the Continental form of *pied de biche* or deer's hoof, introduced, logically enough, in cabriole legs of walnut seat furniture. This design continued in favor through the middle decades of the century, and still later was employed in combination with the delicate marquetry decorations of circa 1785–1790.

If a sequence of designs based on one particular element includes examples of equal importance in other respects, they may be lost to more obvious considerations of different features of design. Therefore, since such presentations can be equally unfeasible or impossible here, an attempt has been made to keep the illustrations as orderly as possible, while comparisons are advised not only between a single category of examples classified as to style, but also between one category and another.

A carved beech and caned side chair, closely related to the lacquer example shown in Ill. 1, has a vertical back panel inlaid with a marquetry floral cartouche; the rear legs are stamped with the initials *E R*. The design of leg in Ill. 2 also appears here in Ill. 34, and in the stand supporting a seaweed marquetry chest of drawers in Macquoid, Pl. X. An armchair with *unusual* stretcher, similar to that in Ill. 4, is said to retain its original needlework covering as shown in Symonds's *Charles II—George II,* Fig. 98. This same stretcher also appears in seat furniture inlaid with characteristic seaweed marquetry panels.

It appears that local marquetry workers were so skilled in their scrolls and flourishes that, like their colleagues' work in gesso, they might be freely offered and accepted as personal monograms. The side chair in Ill. 19 incorporates a cipher identified as that of the Dudley North family, a name which, along with that of DeL'Isle and Dudley and others, will become increasingly familiar in further studies as the original and later owners of the finest specially made Dublin furniture. The shaping of the front leg is quite similar in a gilded gesso upholstered side chair, Macquoid, Fig. 31, owned by the Marquess of Cholmondeley, another name to be remembered. The figured velvet covering of that example may be seen here also in Ill. 21.

Through the courtesy and interest of Temple Williams, the silver gesso upholstered side chair in Ill. 21 is shown in the original velvet covering of a suite comprising six chairs and a pair of stools, specially made for a great English home located in Lancaster, within easy reach of Dublin.

As a very good example of the retention of elements and details favored by Dublin craftsmen, the exact arm support and knee carving—but not the knee shaping—seen in Ill. 26 are both incorporated in a settee with eagle-head arm terminals and claw-and-ball feet (*Dictionary of English Furniture,* Vol. III, Pl. VI). They are also in another settee (*op. cit.* Fig. 24) with the arms of Chetham's Hospital, located in Manchester, which as every schoolboy knows is *situated in the west of England, opposite the east coast of Ireland, almost parallel with its chief port and capital city.*

The splat in Ills. 25 and 26 will also be found in chairs and settees with seat rails centering an unusual type of satyr mask, and with an inversely arched shoe piece in combination with one of the numerous versions of conventionalized hoof feet (Symonds, *Present State,* Pl. XXI), and such as that of the gilded gesso example in Ill. 21, and seen here in Ills. 19 and 20. The open scrolls bracing the front legs of Ill. 20 and appearing also in Ill. 21 are found as well in walnut side tables and highboys of Dublin make. When they are rounded, they also feature the long favored Irish ring leg collar.

Dublin spoon-back writing chairs of the type shown in Ill. 36 sometimes feature a stretcher similar to that of the side chair (Ill. 37) and straddle chair (Ill. 38) (*Charles II—George II,* Fig. 90), a most notable example having its back inlaid with a marquetry scrollwork cartouche with the cipher of the Dudley North family. Straddle chairs (Ill. 38) may have a shallow drawer fitted into the lower portion of the seat, and a hinged desk with ratchet support. A variation of these legs, terminating in a typical Irish trifid foot (one of many variations), appears in Ill. 39, where the treatment of the arm terminal is also characteristic of some Irish work.

The two settees referred to in connection with Ill. 26 have the same eagle-head arm terminal and molded support as the armchair in (Ill. 40), a design that is also found in chair-back settees. The inversely arched and cusped shoe piece of the splat is a favorite Dublin conceit. Another chair-back settee (Ill. 42) is important for the ramped back uprights in which the flat cusped terminals may serve as one form of documentation in classifying Dublin seat furniture with numerous variations of this centrally tied splat, and of the crest, arm, knee, and foot treatments.

Lion-head arm terminals (such as those in Ills. 43 and 47) are more delicately treated in walnut seat furniture than in the heavier examples later produced in mahogany. The back uprights and crest of Fig. 47 were generally less decidedly varied in form with mahogany, although the uprights in Ill. 57 remain pronounced. Chairs similar in design to that shown in Ill. 47, but without its distinctive arms, were produced in padauk, a timber especially favored by Irish joiners.

An American writer has made the general mistake of unknowingly accepting the typical Dublin design of the shepherd's-crook armchair in Ill. 55 as indicating Dutch influence in the working styles of Colonial and Early Federal craftsmen.

An example pointed out by Karl Freund as "Irish as Paddy's pig," and which took me years to prove as such, is the elaborate armchair (Ill. 54) now easily recognized and offered here in all its characteristic features of shaping and carved details. These details echo Freund's description of Irish craftsmen: "What IMAGINATION those fellows had." To which might be added in this instance, "and what a sense of proportion" for such an essay.

Of the few Irish designs whose dates of execution are safely documented, a set of chairs made in 1768 features the shell-and-leaf carving shown in Ills. 59 and 60, so that it may be assumed these two chairs were produced at about the same time. The latter example is not first rate Dublin workmanship, the rear legs are beech—which at least partially explains the worm-riddled frame—and, contrary to rule, there is no separate shoe piece at the base of the splat.

A piece from the Percival Griffiths collection (Ill. 63) is representative of innumerable variations in design, from those of the settee illustrated in Macquoid, Fig. 208, and in the *Dictionary of English Furniture,* Vol. III, Fig. 26, to Ill. 64 here, and to parcel-gilded seat furniture combining eagle-head arm terminals with deer hoofs, similar to the chair-back settee on exhibition at Upton House. Evidence for tracing additional examples is also to be found in the design of Ill. 65, the crest of which features the coat of arms of Sir William Humphreys, Lord Mayor of London. (Macquoid, Fig. 173, owned by Lady North and R. E. Dickson.) A smaller, individual feature—the tassel pendant—as adopted in Early American furniture was inspired by the continued use of this feature by Irish craftsmen (Ills. 67 and 69), who employed it in seat furniture and cabinetwork through the eighteenth and early nineteenth centuries.

Thomas Moore of London supplied a set of ten walnut chairs "with Lyons' faces on ye knees and Lyons' Paws," which have been published as supplied in 1734. The legs of those chairs are quite similar to those of the upholstered side chair (Ill. 73) and the settee (Ill. 74), with distinctive variations that contrast to the lack of variations in Ills. 76–80, and an example said to have been made by Giles Grendey of London on the strength of a label "found beneath a chair" illustrated in *The Age of Mahogany* (Fig. 104). Although various dealers have handled chairs matching this example with the label of Grendey affixed, I know of no instance where that single piece, so labeled, has ever been cited as evidence of such makership.

The typical "wild" Irish armchair (Ill. 76), others of equally distinctive Irish design (*op. cit.* Fig. 106), and the settee (Ill. 77) all display the same knee carving as the scroll-foot chair with the Grendey label attached. The side chair accompanying that armchair (*op. cit.* Fig. 105) matches exactly a set of eight walnut upholstered side chairs formerly owned by Sir Spencer Ponsonby Fane. Each chair of this set is stamped with the initials *W F,* through which the design has been claimed for a later craftsman than Grendey—William France—who worked under Robert Adam's supervision. The Fane chairs are in fact Irish and apparently were among the heirlooms brought along by Sir Spencer and his equally Irish bride when they settled in Brympton D'Enercy, Somerset, where his collection was photographed and published as "English."

The upholstered open-arm easy chair (Ill. 78) may have come from the shop responsible for the Fane side chairs, or possibly from the original suite. It matches the chair with the Grendey label even in the way the leafage of the arm supports is crowded up against the rosette terminals (also see Ill. 80). The other upholstered open-arm easy chair shown in Ill. 79, with the legs ending in paw feet, may be compared with Ill. 76. This chair also features Irish characteristics: its rear legs are embellished, it displays an extra pair of rosette dies at the base of the arm supports, and it makes special use of American black walnut (untouched by the worm although the small beech bracing blocks are riddled).

A further confirmation in respect to the easy chair in Ill. 79 is found in the exact retention of the carved leaf and four-petal rosette terminal of its arm supports, as shown in Symonds's *Charles II–George II,* Fig. 101. This simpler form of hipped knee is also found in chairs incorporating the favorite Irish pierced-beaker splat, and in a later mahogany version of the back treatment featured in the elaborate walnut armchair (Ill. 55). It also appears in tables made either in mahogany or walnut.

Chairs with the palmate back displayed in Ills. 81–84 were plentiful in England when, in 1904, one example was published in an illustration contained in my files bearing the transcribed notation, "24 side chairs and 2 armchairs still at Stourhead. Acquired by owners in early 19th century—6 in Musée Cluny—Design made by Thomas Chippendale for Marie Antoinette" (!!!!).

Dolphins and dolphin heads were continuously favored in Irish seat furniture and tables of Early Georgian and later designs. The wheel back of the example featuring dolphin heads (Ill. 86) is found in combination with elaborately scrolled and cusped shepherd's-crook arms, and with only slightly varied piercing in a later wood-seat armchair of curule or curved "X" formation.

Eagle heads—plain, curved, or with more elaborately shaped necks—were combined with different types of feet in seat furniture, stands, and tables, sometimes with pronounced feathering or scaling on the legs. Scaling was developed in imbrications that came into popular use in corbels and other parts of Early Georgian and Chippendale architectural cabinet pieces and wall mirrors.

One of the most important examples of the Dublin furniture, in which eagle heads are combined with legs incorporating lions' heads and paw feet, is the much publicized settee owned by Lord DeL'Isle and Dudley (Macquoid and *Dictionary of English Furniture*), which has been illustrated in color. The color illustration shows the rich effect of its original Irish needlework covering, which is more important to further studies of Dublin furniture. Along with its matching chairs, and so on, this piece is described as "probably by Giles Grendey."

A chair matching the one represented in Ill. 92, if not the piece itself, has been illustrated since the beginning of this century along with other household items brought over from Ireland to England by Sir Spencer Ponsonby Fane. The handling of the knee in Ill. 93 and the one shown in Ill. 99 will indicate the extra time that Dublin joiners often spent on their individual creations.

Percy Macquoid is responsible for drawing attention to the design of the side chair in Ill. 94, insofar as it is represented in a settee with scrolled eagle-head arm terminals, possibly *en suite,* which he illustrated in his *Age of Walnut* and designated as Irish. He was less sure of a distantly related armchair and settee (Figs. 100 and 101) in his *Age of Mahogany,* but correct in his feeling that they, too, were of Irish provenance.

American furniture collectors may see in the splat of the side chair shown in Ill. 95 one derivation of the patterns employed in this country by Philadelphia joiners. A very close approximation of this splat appeared in "A Queen Anne Shell-Carved Mahogany Drake-Foot Armchair," attributed to William Savery, which sold for four figures in a Parke-Bernet sale of 1958 despite repairs to both rear legs.

The straddle chair in Ill. 97 has a small drawer fitted at the rear of the seat. The important feature for consideration here is the treatment of the knee, which is most characteristic of the Irish school. The knee is often carved with different types of leafage or with a shell, which may also extend up onto the seat rail. Frequently, on either side, more or less pronounced, is the same flaring ribbing or molding as seen in Ills. 102 and 103, while the leg may terminate in a plain or faceted club foot, a slender knuckled version of a lion's paw (Ill. 101), or a plain or heavily webbed claw-and-ball foot. The backs of such seat furniture will range from a reserved pattern close to that of Ill. 23, to more elaborated renditions as in Ill. 101. In Ill. 102 the diagonal ridges at the angles where the back uprights start their ogee curves are also most distinctive.

This same type of leg was used in seat furniture supposedly made for Malahide Castle between 1760 and 1770, and featuring a pierced-beaker splat. While this castle is situated within easy reach of Dublin, many of the examples included in this particular school of design seem to have been produced elsewhere than in the capital, not only because of the designs but, in some instances, from considerations of material and workmanship. Nevertheless, since the designs and working skills of craftsmen employed in any metropolis may vary considerably, it cannot be said at this time that such a possibility is to be ruled out. The truth of this becomes clear in such an example as the carved and inlaid walnut chest-on-stand with ivory claws grasping all four ball feet, owned by the Victoria and Albert Museum. This is a masterpiece that can hardly be classified as suburban, provincial, or "made on the spot," as it has been unknowingly described by one commentator on it.

Restrained Irish designs are represented in Ills. 104 and 106, and in the armchair (Ill. 105) with pierced vasiform splat. However, every single element and detail of this example were produced in many variations. The back uprights might be shaped like those in Ill. 118, the legs enriched with leaf carving on the knees over claw-and-ball feet. Also, rather than surface carving alone, the knees might be deeply cut in shapings approximating those of Ills. 92, 93, and 99; the arms also can undergo numerous variations including the use of eagle-head arm terminals.

Even more prolific were the treatments accorded the favorite pierced-beaker splat in conjunction with crest rail and leg treatments too numerous to mention, often with a rolled and whorled projection at the outside base of the splat, more pronounced than in Ill. 107. Through an illustration published by Cescinsky (Fig. 252) in my clipping files, one such beaker-splat armchair features the same lion-head, paw-foot cabriole legs that appear in the important needlework settee mentioned above in connection with Lord DeL'Isle and Dudley, and attributed to Giles Grendey. This particular example must have been overlooked by those who have so overworked Grendey, for otherwise it might also have been credited to him, along with other Irish beaker-splat seat furniture.

Oak leaves, usually with richer, more clearly defined, effects than seen in Ill. 106, and often with classic arrangements of leaves and acorns as well as grape leaves and clusters of fruit (see Ill. 109), were especially popular in the repertory of Irish furniture carvers in general.

From the very few examples that can safely be associated with dates of execution, it appears that those shown here in Ill. 108, and in the tassel-back chairs of Ills. 113, 114, and 115, were produced between 1760 and 1775.

Collectors of Early American furniture will be acquainted with designs somewhat similar to those of the "New York" and "Pennsylvania" side chairs of Ills. 112 and 114 and those of Ills. 116, 120, and 121, described as "American" without quite such fulsome temerity. The settee with eagle-head arm terminals (Ill. 116) was owned by the Jordan West family of Worcester, Massachusetts. Supposedly, a journeyman from Chippendale's workshop brought over the original designs and specifications from which it was made! This information must have accounted for a selling price of $7,900.

A single chair from a set of six (Ill. 120) is stamped on the rear seat rail with the initials *N C* and has a fleur-de-lis. This set belonged to the John Cabot family of Boston, Massachusetts, eventually descending to Susan E. H. Safford of Fitchburg, Massachusetts. The especially popular Dublin front and rear legs of that design are repeated in the upholstered open-arm easy chair shown in Ill. 126.

The four easy chairs (Ills. 123–126) and two wing chairs (Ills. 127–128) are all Dublin examples of refined quality and distinction: three show a partiality in the use of matching cabriole rear legs; the latter wing chair displays a penchant for treating the knees of seat furniture, stands, and tables with acanthus leafage springing from rosettes.

Knee lappets in numerous forms appear in Irish seat furniture, stands, and tables. One such variation is shown here in Ill. 129. The Dublin bureau-form dressing mirror on this table is typical in the shaping and molding of the frame enclosing the mirror plate. Other dressing or side tables (as well as furniture in general) can be easily distinguished when they are supported on cabriole legs terminating in various versions of the so-called Spanish (but actually Irish) foot (Symonds's *Charles II—George II,* and *passim*). The table in Ill. 132 is of special interest to me since, in outline, it is similar to a decorated red lacquer *toiletborde* of a long-established Danish collection that is believed to have originally "come from England."

American lowboys and the stands of highboys made in New England and New York circa 1750–1770 display the same highly distinctive outline seen in the valanced front of this side table, also with New England type shell carving on the knees. Our debt to Irish designers is usually less apparent in such skirtings or aprons (sometimes furnished with Irish-type finial-like pendants, and other commonly shared features) than in our adoption of baluster-form and cabriole legs, the latter with trifid, trilobate, web, or drake feet, faceted or vertically paneled club feet or drake feet, and also multiple ribbed versions of so-called Spanish feet that were actually derived from Ireland rather than Spain. All such terminals are more determinable as of Irish derivation than our treatments of the plainer cabriole legs, as in Ill. 132, or those ending in webbed or webless claw-and-ball feet.

The favorite Dublin card table with baluster legs (Ill. 134) was more generally produced in semielliptical form, but is also found as a rectangular piece. Legs vary considerably; the top section was eventually fashioned with an incurvate center as in some Dutch examples. The flat stretcher was also widely varied—in one treatment centering in a trilobate section with middle cusp—as in the marquetry cabinet-on-stand from Littlecote (M. Harris's booklet *Old English Furniture,* p. 57) which Symonds published as "Flemish," and in two card tables of the Untermeyer Collection (*Catalogue* 235 and 235) described as "English" ("possibly Continental"). This is a new low in "shotgun" attributions, taking in all the small English towns and the entire European Continent, but still missing its mark by aiming in the wrong direction. It is to be hoped that the Untermeyer Collection will not remain equally blind to the *possibilities* of the needlework shown in Ill. 136, in the illustrations of the DeL'Isle and Dudley settee, chairs, and card table attributed to Grendey, and in those featuring banners of fire screen as shown here and elsewhere.

The Littlecote cabinet mentioned above bears some relationship to the table and cabinet shown in Ills. 138 and 146, and to a cabinet illustrated by Percy Macquoid, *Age of Walnut,* Fig. 50—in particular to the handling of the inlaid scrollwork borders. Closer relationships may be seen in comparing Ills. 139–140 here with Macquoid's side table and chest of drawers (Figs. 46 and 48) and the marquetry chest illustrated in the *Dictionary of English Furniture,* Pl. II. All these pieces are illustrative of the best and most characteristic Dublin marquetry work.

Careful attention to these and other marquetry patterns of the same general type, especially to individual details of foliage and floral treatments and borders, will be rewarding. It will be found that there are no indications of lengthy processes of development between patterns used for so-called William and Mary pieces, and those of cabinets still retaining pulvinar frieze drawers but standing on Early Georgian foliage-carved cabriole legs with claw-and-ball feet, or on other later forms of supports. In their upper sections such pieces will therefore appear earlier than the Queen Anne piece shown here in Ill. 142, but their stands, or at least their legs or feet will prove them actually to be later in date. This is also borne out through cabinets and hanging cabinets of Early Georgian architectural design, which are inlaid with marquetry identical to that shown in the upper and lower frieze drawers of Ills. 139–140. A good example of William and Mary oyster-parquetry and border work, combined with plain cabriole legs in a late Queen Anne piece, appears here in Ill. 146.

With another Dublin favorite—the slant-front bureau-on-stand—designs may be traced from examples with spiral-turned legs, through baluster forms also employed for card tables and the taller cabinet pieces, to later cabriole forms as in the dressing bureau (Ill. 143). Especially favored in these walnut bureaus, the trilobate, tricleft, or drake foot of Ill. 145 is unmistakably Irish and appears in some of the finest Dublin pieces.

The upper, slant-front portion of these bureaus may overhang the rest at front and sides without necessarily indicating earlier work, which is sometimes true with respect to larger bureaus and bureau-cabinets. Later, when these smaller bureaus and dressing bureaus were fashioned in mahogany as well as in walnut, the general design was retained in combination with elaborately carved features such as lion or satyr masks, foliage clusters, paw feet, and so on.

The bureau with arcaded stand (Ill. 144) has been of particular interest to these studies. Labeled as "Dutch, William and Mary, Circa 1690," the appearance of pine in its carcass work belied such provenance. A crucial clue in tracing the design was provided by the baluster-form legs. Later, the original handles and escutcheon helped in identifying other types of Dublin cabinetwork.

The plainness of the pedestal desk in Ill. 147 has allowed it to be styled as Queen Anne, although other quite similar and genuine antique examples with brasses or border inlays of obviously later patterns have received circa dates of 1710–1730, which are also fallacious.

A learned European authority has contrasted the Continental habit of supplying drawers of equal depths for commodes (chest of drawers), bureaus, secretaires, and so on with the English custom of fitting such pieces with drawers of graduated depths. This, of course, is a rule of thumb, and there will inevitably be exceptions in practice as well as in plates published by London designers. However, in work influenced by the French school, or styled in Germany, Denmark, Flanders, Italy, and so on, it is generally true that full-length drawers are of equal depths. Holland, however, is a principal exception to this rule. While there were variations, drawers produced in Holland were generally graduated.

It will be of some interest and possible value to keep this observation in mind, especially with respect to Dublin cabinetwork executed in walnut, but also in regard to mahogany examples, solid or veneered, displaying elaborate foreign effects. Furthermore, it will be helpful to collectors of British furniture to remember this Continental practice when a Dresden secretaire of remarkably fine quality with lower drawers of even depths is exhibited and sold as "A Treasure of English Art."

Dutch influence was not introduced into the production of Early American furniture with great sophistication. However, it is clearly apparent in the exterior designs, interior fittings, and frequent and selective choice of oak as a secondary material (for this was a required use in Holland) of Dublin bureau-cabinets or secretaires that Dutch artisans were successfully employed in Dublin during the popularity of Queen Anne designs.

It should be understood by now that the influence so long accepted in America as having come from Holland was in fact derived from the development of native and foreign designing and technical skills in Dublin. These foreign influences resulted, in part, from an influx of artisans from Denmark and northern Germany, whose presence becomes especially apparent in examples of Early Georgian designs and later in those featuring elaborate marquetry effects.

The finer Dublin secretaires with decided Dutch influence will invariably display the Dutch preference for fitting the underbody with drawers of graduated depths. In the examples shown here (Ills. 149–150), the interior fittings of the upper section are of fine quality straight-grained oak, and oak appears again in the carcass work with a partial use of pine. As a deviation from Continental practice in general, the double-astragal, or twin-bead molding, is used to finish off the lower drawer framings.

In Dublin kneehole or pedestal-form dressing and writing tables, in walnut or lacquer, the banks of small drawers are *usually* of equal depths. But, while following a Continental propensity in this respect, such pieces are generally devoid of foreign effects and were obviously designed and produced by native or locally trained artisans. This type of dressing table remained in favor despite the rising popularity of mahogany and the continued use of walnut in Ireland during the vogue of Chippendale designs. Occasional examples are found in satinwood, still produced in Queen Anne and Early Georgian designs.

In the secretaire with shallow cornice (Ill. 152) and "no frieze" (as constantly noted in these studies of Dublin cabinetwork in walnut and mahogany), the underbody is completely fashioned in one form of these kneehole dressing tables, which appear with two or four front bracket feet. The same brasses with which this piece is furnished are commonly found on such tables, and also in larger cabinetwork.

The Dublin secretaire of Ill. 154 is important for its handles and escutcheons, as well as its hinges, finials, and other details. For years its photograph was compared with Continental examples and others that seemed remotely English. It is shown here in place of numerous other examples of its type with less clearly defined identifying details. Similar examples also appear with either single or double flat-arched crestings (see Ill. 151) in secretaires and cabinet pieces on stands with baluster-form legs or cabriole legs, even with claw-and-ball feet. The example shown in Ill. 155 is of equal documentary value, shown here under Queen Anne rather than Early Georgian because of the favorite central coved recess of the base, with its stellate inlay so commonly found in Dublin cabinetwork of Queen Anne and later periods.

In addition to kneehole chests, the bachelor chest was also favored in Dublin but did not remain so long in popularity. The earlier inlaid walnut chests of drawers might be mounted on stands lower than those with cabriole supports, or follow the more usual form (Ill. 158), a blanket chest, a type favored in America, whose hinged top opens to a full-length well. A typical Dublin piece in all respects, this fine example was acquired by a discriminating collector who then was told that it was "not English but Portuguese."

Dublin examples similar to Ill. 159 have attracted misinformed critics who have claimed that the molding that serves as a cornice indicates that such a piece was originally the top section of a chest-on-stand or chest-on-chest. It has also been said that such marquetry veneer applied to bracket feet has been removed from a lower section or part of another piece. The sides of these front bracket feet are of unveneered oak with original patination; the carcass, including dust boards, is of oak; and the piece is entirely original throughout including handles and escutcheons.

Early walnut bookcases or china cabinets might also be mounted on low stands (as is the piece illustrated in Macquoid, Fig. 19), while occasional examples are found with doors overlapping in a central *meet*. In this structural method, both inside framing members are chamfered along their meeting edges so that one overlays the other when closed, a phenomenon to be observed more frequently in later Dublin cabinetwork. Bookcases similar to the one shown in Ill. 161 were also made with lower banks of drawers, either graduated or of equal depth, while very similar early designs were executed in mahogany.

Another of these bookcases appears in Ill. 162. Here an early and possibly original owner had the capacity increased by having wings added. That this took place well before our modern studies of antiques, "perhaps in the George II period," as Mr. Stamp has pointed out, "is quite obvious in the piece itself" and in the veneers of the center doors, which are straight-grained walnut, while those of the end doors display a contrasting wavy figure as though the craftsman tried to outdo his predecessor in this one respect.

The fielded effect of the panels appearing in the narrow walnut cabinet (Ill. 163) is reminiscent of seventeenth-century work in oak. This same treatment is found in Dublin wardrobes, suggesting that, in this instance, the arched crest framing a festooned flaming-urn finial is more in keeping with the later Baroque designs of northern Europe.

A plentitude of Irish wine coolers has given rise to the term *jardiniere* for these brass-bound conveniences. Decanter stands appear in Early Georgian designs, but cellarettes were more popular in Chippendale and later styles. As previously observed, Irish craftsmen displayed a great deal of ingenuity in designing aids to comfort and good cheer, as the stand in Ill. 164 proves. Here the favorite Irish knee lappet has been outlined with a raised molding. It is more prominent here than in Ill. 165 where the three-quarter gallery displays another favored use: pierced handgrips combined with one of many card-cut fret patterns.

Triangular drop-leaf tables were popular in walnut as well as mahogany. The faceted or vertically paneled club foot of the example here (Ill. 167), representing a much favored treatment, with numerous variations in Irish seat furniture, stands, and tables, was adopted in American pieces of the same general type.

An earlier design, anticipatory of the tray-top table, is featured in the light-toned mahogany center table (Ill. 168), which is unlikely to have been made before 1725–1735 when mahogany first came into popular use in English furniture. This is some time later than the circa date of 1710 that has been associated with the one published example applied with a label of Hugh Granger, whose death has been recorded as prior to August 24, 1706.

The oyster parquetry that appears in the center table (Ill. 171) confirms that Dublin craftsmen were carrying on this type of veneering during the middle decades of the eighteenth century. The wide cross-grained molding, framing three sides of the frieze drawer, is also typical of such work.

Irish craftsmen also produced some gaming tables with fixed top rather than folding top sections, various types of architects' drawing tables, flat-top table desks, and, of course, the more accommodating pedestal desk, which appears in many forms. The Dublin library writing table belonging to the Duke of Beaufort, Badminton House, Gloucestershire, and attributed to Thomas Chippendale (*Georgian Cabinet-Makers,* Pl. 102), draws attention to a whole series of kneehole, pedestal, and commode forms of library pieces such as Ills. 172 and 173, types that are generally attributed to either William Vile, circa 1740 (*op. cit.* Pl. 55), or to Chippendale, circa 1750. The number and variety of these Dublin examples—in contrast to those safely known to actually have been made in London (*one* is shown *op. cit.* Pl. 90)—seems to confirm a considerable preponderance of fine Dublin work in comparison with that of the English capital.

Another of these library tables, said to have been made "circa 1735," for the second Duke of Montague, and until 1917 at Montague House, Whitehall, has been illustrated by Oliver Bracket, from the collection of the Duke of Buccleuch, who had a taste for Irish furniture not always of the finest quality. In that example, a median fret frieze is so faulty that it would never have been acceptable to a London shop master. A closely related, but more finished, design, featuring "Vile and Cobb" type oval panels with leaf clasps, has been illustrated as from the Sir Alfred Beit Collection—without mention that this collection, at Rossborough House, is located in Ireland.

Attributed to Thomas Chippendale, the Dublin folding-top writing table in Ill. 172 is similar in design to the "Kent school of furniture" (R. W. Symonds, *Charles II—George II,* Fig. 129). Another of the numerous developments of this library piece, featuring bowknoted pendants of fruit and foliage (*Dictionary of English Furniture,* Fig. 11), from Rokeby Park, Yorkshire, is additionally enhanced with the same type of oval panel moldings interrupted by leaf clasps and pilasters as those of Ill. 173. These oval panels, rosette dies, and scrolled brackets were also employed in combination with pilasters capped by cherub heads, as in a library table formerly in the Earl of Shaftesbury's collection and considered possibly the work of Benjamin Goodison. A satyr mask was the central feature of a semioctagonal desk of this class, formerly owned by Her Majesty Queen Mary and sold in the Chrysler sale, Parke-Bernet Galleries, at $6,000.

The so-called Dublin diner with deep drop leaves hinged to a narrow central slab over straight or cabriole supports is no more representative of capital-city work in general than are the more sophisticated drop-leaf tables made of oak (Macquoid, Ill. 48). A refined Dublin example is shown in Ill. 174, with rich foliage carving and vigorous molding of the upper legs, in which the tapered lower portion is characteristically grooved and finished with a superior claw-and-ball foot. The triple molding around the top edge is indicative of a considerably later date than circa 1745, usually associated with designs of this general description.

Smaller Dublin dining tables that preceded the pedestal types were often oval drop-leaf pieces with cabriole legs ending in the Irish pointed club foot, the rudimentary web or drake foot, the claw-and-ball, or other types of paw feet. One of the most favored, however, was the hoof foot (Ill. 176). The retention of individually favored elements for long periods of time in Irish furniture, even in the capital, is evidenced in the continued use of the hoof foot, combined with Dublin marquetry of classic scrollwork, in pieces of typically Hepplewhite design.

Early Georgian side tables of the lowboy type (Ill. 177) were furnished with all forms of legs and feet used in the preceding tables; this also applies to card tables. In the smaller, half-round card tables, the fixed and hinged top sections of walnut examples still featured the concave edge treatment of earlier examples with baluster-form legs (see Ill. 134).

The leg of the Dublin card table (Ill. 180) is duplicated in chairs, chair-backed and upholstered settees, sometimes with the identical center ornament of the seat rail. The leg in Ill. 181, and its pendanted front rail, is also duplicated in seat furniture (Symonds, *Charles II— George II*, Fig. 30). In a comparison of these two tables with one bearing the label of Benjamin Crook, London (Symonds *passim*), the latter comes out a very poor third in terms of design, carving, and appeal or charm.

In the two card tables in Ills. 182 and 187, despite the use of walnut in the former and an earlier shaping of its top portion, the legs of both pieces are much alike and display the same type of Dublin "V-" notched leaf carving on their knees. Those of the five-legged table with multiple lids (Ill. 183) are also similarly carved and notched. Coming from a collection in Russia, where David Roentgen traveled by van with examples of his work, this table was once considered one of his productions as an *"Englischer Kabinettmacher."*

Laburnum, as a medium of the cabinetmaker, became increasingly important as piece after piece in these showy veneers continued to display characteristics of Irish design. From the number of tables that employ Chippendale fret or other related treatments in combination with the straight cabriole leg as shown in Ill. 184, it is clear that such legs were in vogue during the development of the Chippendale style. The same leg also appears in a Dublin half-round card table of padauk, inlaid with a leaf-scroll design in mother-of-pearl.

I took the photograph used for Ill. 185 with me on a visit to Amsterdam and Copenhagen where leading authorities believed the piece to have probably been the work of a Dutch cabinetmaker; one, no doubt, among those employed in the Irish capital.

In addition to the DeL'Isle and Dudley lion-mask, paw-foot card table, another variation should be recognized as typical of fine Dublin craftsmanship. This has been published by R. W. Symonds and also appears in the *Dictionary of English Furniture,* Fig. 25. In the Percival Griffiths collection it was accompanied by two Dublin settees with legs that matched it, but with varying designs of their splats (*op. cit.* Fig. 27 and Cescinsky *passim*).

A popular Dublin design with numerous minor variations, the table in Ill. 187 was produced in both walnut and mahogany, with the gadroons of the frieze as customary, slanting away from the center ornament, as well as running in opposite directions (see Ill. 193). In a famous collection of American furniture, this table was believed to be an example of Philadelphia craftsmanship.

The legs of the side tables in Ills. 188 and 189 may be compared to those of the spoon-back writing chair (Ill. 44) and the card table (Ill. 180) where the center ornament also appears, as it does in the well known walnut and gilt settee from the Marquess of Cholmondeley, Houghton Hall (Macquoid, and so on). Other tables with the same frieze shaping and molding were made in Virginia walnut, with paw feet, masks, etc., somewhat similar in design but varying in certain ways from the one in R. W. Symonds's *Charles II–George II*, Fig. 178.

The identical leg of Ill. 189, combined with a similar frieze treatment in which the center cartouche features a female mask, appeared in a walnut stool owned by Percival Griffiths. When the Griffiths collection was dispersed, the stool was classified by British authorities of the Inland Revenue as an Article of National Interest. Another Dublin treatment in which the rail centers a winged satyr mask is illustrated in R. W. Symonds's *Charles II–George II*, Fig. 12.

The basic design of Ill. 191 appears in numerous Dublin side tables, with special attention to the shaping of the apron and its central shell ornament.

Dublin tables of various types feature the leg treatment shown in Ill. 192. The piece displays such relatively light oxidation and patination that it must have been produced some years later than its design would seem to indicate—sometimes the case with Dublin seat furniture as well as cabinetwork. Another typical leg treatment is shown in Ill. 193 along with an unmistakable Irish stool.

Early Georgian, Chippendale, and later styles are combined in the side or pier table in Ill. 194. Here the shaping of the knee, foot, the tied leaf clasp of the knee, the frieze band, and the heavily reeded edge are all important in considerations of Dublin designs. The frieze may be compared with the foliated fret employed on the legs of the lacquer cabinet-on-stand (Ill. 238).

The plainer and usually smaller versions of these Dublin pier tables appear among collections of Early American furniture, frequently in deeper rather than lighter tones of mahogany, with club, drake, or claw-and-ball feet. The frieze is generally plain, but there may be some ornamentation such as gadrooning, foliage, or shell carving along the lower edge, which may also appear on the knees. These examples, of course, have been acquired as representative of the work of Philadelphia craftsmen.

Since it has been acknowledged that pieces known to have been contained in Irish homes may be considered as having originated in that country, it is odd that long accepted authorities seem never to have considered this possibility in respect to the "Black Lacquer Cabinet decorated with bouquets of flowers in natural colours," circa 1745 (from the Dowager Duchess of Limerick), illustrated in the *Dictionary of English Furniture*, Fig. 22. The cabinet section of this Dublin piece proves the origin of its gesso table stand, just as its stand proves the origin of the cabinet. Both are helpful in classifying many other gesso tables and similarly decorated cabinet pieces.

Gesso side tables such as the two outstanding examples shown in Ills. 195 and 196, and others with legs ending in different types of hooves, paws, scrolls, dolphin heads, and so on—including some with plumed red-Indian or satyr masks as leg capitals—had their top surfaces carved with elaborate arabesque panels centering interlacements, which, crowned or uncrowned, may be accepted as royal or other monograms (Macquoid, Fig. 26, from the Duke of Devonshire). In one group of these side tables, the same type of open-scroll brackets appears as those developed in the supports of the side chair in Ill. 21. (See also *Dictionary of English Furniture*, Fig. 19.)

The classic form of scrolled support carved with acanthus and imbrications (see Ill. 198) appears in side tables, often late in date, with the marble slab projecting or inset in characteristic Irish fashion. For an example, see Macquoid, Fig. 20, which is owned by the Marquess of Cholmondeley. Variations of this leg also occur in the stands of cabinets, such as the one of architectural design (*op. cit.* Fig. 90) owned by the Duke of Marlborough, and believed "originally" to have come from Blenheim.

An outstanding example of imaginative design is the Dublin console (Ill. 199). This type of table was also fashioned with the frieze centering a festooned human or animal mask.

Eagle consoles like the one represented in Ill. 200, which R. W. Symonds illustrated along with the example in Ill. 201, has been claimed by him to be "the work of a London craftsman of the first rank." "The best English carving" of "circa 1700" was claimed by Percy Macquoid for another console owned by Lady North and R. Eden Dickson. As a matter of easily determined fact, these consoles are considerably later in date than generally believed. As they continued to be produced during and after the turn of the eighteenth century, they often lacked quality and spontaneity, as two varying examples (*op. cit.* Figs. 14 and 15) owned by the Duke of Beaufort, Badminton House, Gloucestershire show. The opposite is true of the highly finished Dublin design in Ill. 202, of which several less perfect variations have been published.

A Dublin kneehole chest with canted pilasters similar to those of Ill. 204 is shown in R. W. Symonds's *Charles II—George II,* Fig. 60. The handles of these kneehole chests are a favorite Irish pattern, and both examples support Irish dressing mirrors.

From such Irish examples as the chest-on-chest (Ill. 205) and the child's bureau (Ill. 207A), it would seem that speculations on the original source of blockfront designs in American furniture have now been settled for once and all. E. M. Bingham, Jr., was amused at the interest that dealers in American furniture displayed in this piece that he had obtained in original condition, including the handles and escutcheons, "in the West Country region of England." A varied blockfront shaping is shown in the example illustrated by Percy Macquoid (*Age of Walnut,* Fig. 137), along with the comment, "nationality not clearly defined."

The interior treatment of the Dublin secretaire with glass finials (Ill. 210) is very close to those appearing in Dutch and Irish examples with double-arched crests. A transitional development, with five finial figures, is illustrated in the *Dictionary of English Furniture,* Fig. 23, and Cescinsky, 186–187. Other important features for further classification are the double-panel borders of the lower drawer fronts, and the central-shaped panel with mirror plate inset of the crest. Less likely to be of such service are the spired globe finials of glass, where one Irish craft has called upon another for an additional display of imagination and creativeness.

A number of Dublin secretaires, which may have been designed and executed by German craftsmen employed in Ireland, have been described as once owned by the King or the Prince of Saxony. Through the study of Dublin pier mirrors, these pieces, in walnut and in lacquer, have been confirmed as of the same provenance. Therefore, one such example is shown here in Ill. 211. I have since been informed by a German dealer in antique furniture that the royal family of Saxony was known for collecting antique silver, but had little interest in antique furniture, "English" or otherwise.

Regardless of the very fine work produced in Saxony, Genoa, Copenhagen, or Amsterdam, nothing can surpass the secretaire presented in Ill. 212. It is difficult not to indulge in superlatives. Under magnification, one can see that a very delicate border, repeatedly referred to in these studies as the "Dublin *open* bead-and-billet-chain banding," appears in the facings of the interior small drawers, pediment, pilaster panels, slant lid, and exterior drawers. To designate such an example as "English" is simply amateurish, since it is obviously representative of the finest possible Dublin work. No other European city could have produced such a masterpiece.

In all respects, the legs of the stand supporting the parquetry cabinet (Ill. 217) are typical of Dublin carving. This applies also to the shell-centered festoons of the frieze, where it appears as though the artisan may have turned on impulse from carving grapes or berries to producing blossoms, or vice versa. The rosette dies, corbels, and slender vine pendants of the collector's cabinet, along with similar lower recessed panels with applied rosettes at the incurvate corners (Ill. 218), are found in other Dublin cabinets of varying sizes up to large breakfront bookcases. That combination is repeated and enlarged upon in Ill. 219, which has been considered representative of the designing and carving skills of William Vile, thus adding to his known work a new penchant for satyr masks combined with scaling! This cabinet is one of a pair described by R. W. Symonds as made by Vile and Cobb, circa 1750, and presented by King George IV to Admiral Vavasseur. The same corbels and vine pendants appear on the canted stiles of other Dublin case pieces, and also on the irregular, carved panel moldings applied to the cupboard doors.

One of the greatest Dublin cabinets of architectural design (Ill. 220) is presented here through the aid of Christopher Gilbert, keeper of Temple Newsam, and the cooperation of magnificent example is obviously from the same shop that produced the one illustrated in Peter Thornton, keeper of the department of furniture, Victoria and Albert Museum. This M. Harris's booklet *Old English Furniture,* p. 42, from the Earl of Charlemont, Charlemont House, Dublin. Both pieces are outstanding accomplishments, unexcelled in any of the capitals of Europe. A more heavily carved example, also from the collection of the late C. D. Rotch, was illustrated by R. W. Symonds, in an article entitled "Unknown Georgian Cabinet-Makers." In his latest, and most extravagant, work, he illustrated a plain version, as "possibly" by the maker of the museum's piece (Symonds, Fig. 180).

Interior fittings of the secretaire-cabinet (Ill. 221) are more characteristically Irish than the exterior design, which features the favored range of shallow drawers beneath the cupboard doors, opening on hinges extending over the width of the pilasters.

A typically Irish treatment is the carving of mullions and the inner edges of their framings with an echinus molding, especially in china cabinets and bookcases. Such carving appears in provincial designs as well as in those obviously of capital-city production. It is represented here in Ill. 222. The brasses, however, are more important to notice in this example, as they are in Ill. 223, where the escutcheons and handles are more noticeably Irish than the fitted writing drawer with deep pullout supporting slides below, or the shape of the bracket feet. These same handles appear frequently in both walnut and mahogany cabinets, secretaires, and chests of drawers, and were used, along with numerous other Irish patterns, by Early American cabinetmakers in their choice of handles and escutcheons. The escutcheons in Ill. 223 are a particularly popular Dublin pattern, which also appears in the bookcase of the magazine article referred to above.

Architectural cabinets of designs related to those shown in Ills. 224 and 225 appear in numerous variations. One owned by the Duke of Marlborough (Macquoid, *Age of Mahogany,* Fig. 90) is precariously supported on a tall seven-legged Irish stand; another (Fig. 98) displays an intricate rosetted fret border that is a duplication of one featured in a Dublin side table of the late eighteenth century. This may be of some help in securing more accurate circa dates for these pieces. A further aid in this respect may be found in the use of certain patterns of Irish handles with which some examples are fitted. One example is a set used for a cabinet illustrated in the *Dictionary of English Furniture,* Fig. 29, and is also found in Irish pieces made of padauk and laburnum, as well as in others finished in lacquer.

All the cabinets of this type that I have seen are later than the circa dates with which they have been associated. The one shown in Ill. 224 was recorded by R. W. Symonds as "Originally (*sic*) at Stowe, one time the seat of the Duke of Buckingham," and "from the design of William Kent . . . 1730–1740." Symonds complained that in the catalogue of the New York auction in which this piece was sold "no mention was made of the interesting history of this cabinet. That it came from Stowe—a mansion where William Kent not only carried out landscape gardening and the design of temples in the grounds, but also designed parts of the house and its interior, following after Vanbrugh—was ignored. Now, however, knowing that this cabinet has some connection with Kent it is permissible to ascribe its design to him. . . . If I had not known Miss Manson and visited her house at Bedford, I should never have been able to place on record the original (*sic*) home of this cabinet—which, from the point of view of the furniture student, would have been a sad loss. The fact that it is now no longer anonymous puts it into a different category from the majority of pieces of English furniture."

As a long accepted authority and writer on the *construction* of supposedly "English" furniture, R. W. Symonds had completely failed to understand the very late structural techniques employed in the manufacture of this Irish cabinet. Although it is antique, and bid in for $500 by a most knowledgeable trade friend who otherwise would not have touched it at any price, the piece is much closer in date to circa 1800 than to Symonds's "1730–1740."

Among the huge shipments of furniture Karl Freund was bringing out of Ireland during the opening decades of the present century to supply his galleries and private clients, and to make up collections that were sold by the leading auction house of his time, were so-called Charles II decorated lacquer cabinets on carved and gilded stands. The oldest-appearing of these stands were stretchered, with feet ending in upswept leaf scrolls, and openwork aprons frequently featuring cupids, singly or as a pair, holding a basket of flowers.

Among the pieces shipped as private cargo at approximately the same time and included in the household effects brought from Ireland to England by the Irish nobleman Sir Spencer Ponsonby Fane and his Irish wife were the same types of cabinets with similar and varying stands (Macquoid, Figs. 127 and 131). Aquatic birds, which are included in the decoration of a Fane cabinet, are seen again in a similar cabinet owned by the Duke of Beaufort, Badminton House, Gloucestershire, which is supported on a stand with spiral-turned front supports (*op. cit.* 129–130).

Another of these cabinets (*op. cit.* Figs. 1–2), owned by Viscount Enfield, one of the early collectors of Irish furniture, displays the same type of antlered *foo lions* that were featured in one of Karl Freund's imports, and appear here in the secretaire (Ill. 240).

Because of their Baroque appearance, these stands were considered to represent seventeenth-century work. This supposition was then extended to the cabinets they were made to support. Such stands must have drawn attention away from the cabinets themselves, for it is difficult to understand how a lack of age commensurate with such a date could have continuously gone unnoticed up to the present time.

A mahogany side table of Early Georgian design, but with typical Chippendale ribbon-and-rosette carved lower frieze molding (Cescinsky 134), features similarly carved and pierced foliage with eagles, cherubs, and a central cartouche. This piece has apparently gone unnoticed by the accepted authorities, as has the appearance of similarly carved stands supporting Chinese cabinets obviously of Ch'ien Lung or later dates.

The decoration of the cabinet in Ill. 227 is quite similar to the decoration of the one in Ill. 228, which is surmounted by a Chippendale fret gallery in which the posts and knob finials, and the central dipped portion, approximate the features of the Badminton House commode-cabinet, Ills. 229 and 420. A study of the decorations applied to these cabinets, and the examples that follow, will give some idea of the achievements in this large field of Dublin furniture.

Early examples of Dublin seat furniture with lacquer decoration are shown in Ills. 1, 2, and 16, while the general design of Ill. 20 was also followed in this medium. Lacquer case pieces range from small side tables with drawers (Ill. 235) through kneehole dressing chests and their mirrors, to chests-on-stands and single or double chests of drawers, which, in some instances, were given the blockfront shapings later introduced in New England. The reverse of these convex shapings appears in a series of recesses rising vertically to coved headings, as in the example illustrated both by Macquoid and Ellwood, as the property of Viscountess Wolseley.

The rich floral decoration of a Dublin bureau-cabinet (Ill. 236) and the sectional view of a secretaire (Ill. 241) are related to varying urns of blossoms featured in cabinets supported on carved and gilded stands of the Baroque type, as well as to the example owned by the Dowager Duchess of Limerick.

All details of the painted decoration seen in the cabinet section of Ill. 238 are as important to these studies as the form and relief ornamentation of its stand. Similarly valuable for their landscape and water vignettes, figures, birds, and remarkable animals are the examples shown in Ills. 239, 240, and 242, which have been grouped here to typify this type of Dublin artistry.

Secretaires were especially popular in lacquer decoration (Symonds and Ormsby, Pl. XXXVIII, and Symonds *passim*). One owned by Lord DeL'Isle and Dudley (Macquoid, Fig. 132) displays favorite Dublin interior effects (Ill. 242), as well as the combination of arched pediment with valanced base, and a Chinese type of handle found on Irish pieces made in mahogany, padauk, and laburnum.

A Chippendale settee from Bramshill Park, Hampshire (Macquoid, Fig. 34), and a side chair from that suite (Ill. 284) may be compared with the chair in Ill. 247, in which the carving of the cabriole legs, particularly in relation to the inside scroll (see Ill. 269), the horizontal C-scroll just beneath the seat rail (*op. cit.* Fig. 114), and the use of reverse gadrooning are all characteristic Irish treatments. The same C-scroll appears again in Ill. 248, and in Ill. 249 where the scaled lower portion of the leg terminates in a dolphin's head, a feature employed both in seat furniture (Macquoid, Fig. 175) and tables of Dublin origin. A ribbon-back chair with dolphin feet was illustrated by Cescinsky (Fig. 186) next to a tripod table with dolphin legs (Fig. 187), which he dated "circa 1755–60" despite its late Regency pillar. It would be interesting if an expert on antique furniture could examine this table, to determine whether it may actually date from around 1830.

Further examples of this fanciful and often extravagant school of carving are shown in illustrations 255, 256, and 257. The armchair in Ill. 255 features the favorite Dublin frill running along the edge of the back uprights, and an Irish handling of the arm terminal, which is more embellished in Ill. 256. A more pronounced use of this frill appears in the crest portion of the ribbon-back model (Ill. 257), where the favorite Irish tassel pendant has been omitted (see Ill. 292). It may never be determined whether or not that greatest of all plagiarists Thomas Chippendale was acquainted with such Dublin ribbon-back designs, some of which might well have been developed a decade or more after he had wrongfully published so many bona fide French designs as his own. It is unlikely, however, that he could have produced more successful interpretations. A modified version of the foot appearing in Ill. 257 is shown in Ill. 258, where the crest centers an incipient ribbed canopy-like ornamentation that will be more fully developed in the illustrations of Chinese Chippendale seat furniture.

The handling of the back shown in the armchair (Ill. 277), which has been incorrectly designated as "American," is found in combination with various types of cabriole legs, and with an arm similar to that in Ill. 285. A chair-back settee of this general design, with beech rails, has been similarly claimed as the work of Benjamin Randolph of Philadelphia. The chair-back appearing in Ill. 278 was also combined with different types of richly carved cabriole legs, and, in some instances, with gadrooning along the seat rails. A splat similarly employed in seat furniture with cabriole legs, sometimes with arm terminals overhanging scrolled supports faced with the typical Dublin slender ribbed leaf carving, appears in Ill. 296. Here the usual tassel pendant has been exchanged for a carillon of fifteen bells.

Ribbon-back chairs with straight legs, as in Ill. 292, are generally furnished with recessed stretchers, even if the front legs are of the form seen in Ill. 298, where the rear supports and their terminals are also characteristic of Dublin work.

In dealing with the Bramshill Park suite, and another of the same design from Shire End, Perthshire (Scotland), R. W. Symonds claimed that both "unquestionably signify the skilled craftsmanship of the London chairmaker; one of high standing in the trade with many customers both in town and country." The numerous customers of Dublin furniture makers have already been mentioned.

Developments leading up to the design shown in Ill. 299, employing various types of French cabriole legs (Macquoid, Fig. 186), indicate that Dublin joiners were soon to be producing more typical Hepplewhite designs, as illustrated in Ills. 295 and 302. The splat of the latter example appears in a chair-back settee illustrated by Cescinsky and others, with claw-and-ball arm terminals.

The great preponderance of Dublin furniture designs, in proportion to those produced in London, is again obvious in regard to the many different examples of Dublin, or Irish, ladder-back chairs. It would take far more room than space allows to cover adequately the multiplicity of forms and patterns included in this one category. Examples selected for presentation here will give some idea of developments leading up to and including so-called Adam and Hepplewhite effects.

Imagination is again reflected in the designs of Pl. 138. The ribbon-back armchair (Ill. 313) is remarkable not only for its varied interlacements, but for the molding work of all its frame members, except the smooth quadrangular rear supports with their characteristic splayed terminals. The flamelike leafage of the splat, which is commonly found in Dublin tables as well as seat furniture, recalls similar treatments in work of the Hansa towns of northern Germany. Flamelike effects are repeated as spires in Ills. 314 and 315. The distinctive terminals of the crest rail in Ill. 315 also appear in Irish chairs of more provincial character.

Chinese Chippendale seat furniture (Ills. 316–324) had not received particular attention in my research until I noticed that they constantly appeared in collections and advertisements of the leading Scottish dealer in antique furniture. By 1950, the blind-fret carving, cluster-column legs, and equally typical ornamental corner brackets, appearing in other types of Irish seat furniture, silver tables, and so on, made it possible to classify this other large category as of Dublin design.

At about that time I was asked to look at an armchair of a design closely related to that of the Dublin example in Ill. 316. The problematical piece, obviously of British design, did not seem to possess an aging commensurate with the usually assigned circa date of 1760. I explained that a time lapse usually accounts for this in certain examples of fairly late eighteenth-century Irish furniture. The chair, of the same design as a set made for the Connock family, Trewergey Manor, Cornwall, was then catalogued by the late Leslie A. Hyam as "Irish, Early XIX Century." That date, while certainly not quite fair to the chair or its consignor, reflected the obviously well considered opinion of an expert with many years of experience in the examination of antique furniture from all parts of the world.

The armchair in Ill. 317 is described as being of beech veneered with walnut and sycamore. Veneers appearing on the rear uprights and side seat rails have the appearance of laburnum. Beech also appears in the frame of the side chair in Ill. 320, in contrast to the problematical piece mentioned above showing various well-defined signs of age.

In Ill. 324, the legs and their blockings, together with the matching lower "bamboo" member of the seat rail, are similar to a Dublin cellarette (Jourdain and Rose, Fig. 164), where these blockings are considered *unusual*. Such effects, however, are quite common in typically Irish silver tables.

Formerly owned by Governor John Wentworth of New Hampshire, the settee in Ill. 323 was confiscated and sold at auction in 1776 by the federal government. Thus, it has become a piece of well recorded evidence of Dublin furniture received in the colonies prior to the American Revolution. When the clustered ribbings of the back and seat rail are compared with the same ornamentation on the tall posts of the Chinese Chippendale bedstead from Badminton House (Ill. 367), it provides partial evidence of additional exportation from Dublin. Of the many examples published by Percy Macquoid and generally overlooked for their documentary value, a typical example of Chinese Chippendale seat furniture, in lacquer, and with a most characteristic Irish choice of eagle-head arm terminals, appears as Fig. 14 in his invaluable *Age of Mahogany*.

Upholstered chairs were also supplied in suites of Chinese Chippendale design. With such frames, the front legs might be wider and more elaborately pierced than in the pair shown in Pl. 144. The blind, or unpierced, fret pattern of the stool in the same plate (and the C-brackets) were also popular in the ornamentation of table legs. This is true also in respect to the scrolling leafage and brackets of the armchair in the same illustration.

In an auction sale some years back, the armchair (Ill. 329), which Horner had illustrated in his *Blue Book, Philadelphia Furniture,* was offered as "by Thomas Affleck of Philadelphia." Sometime between its arrival in this country and its appearance at auction, it had acquired a formidable pedigree. This included ownership by William Penn, and, if that were not enough to stir the heart of any American collector, ownership also by George Washington. As this pedigree seemed exaggerated, even in relation to similar stories handed down to collectors of supposedly American furniture, a photograph was obtained and placed in my files. For years that print remained inactive, but finally, through the computerized method of classification that I have followed, the chair was proved in all respects to be of pure Dublin design. It had never been considered as an American piece, least of all as one produced by Thomas Affleck, whose working style did not even closely approximate that of the actual maker.

Irish needlework, which is a most interesting study, often features a basket of flowers, a theme much favored in the carving of Irish furniture, pier mirrors, and overmantels. Outstanding examples of this craft have already been mentioned in the coverings of the famous suite of lion-mask seat furniture owned by Lord DeL'Isle and Dudley. That same needlework, featuring a floral border framing a country landscape with figures of humans and animals, appears in the oval panel of a pole screen whose base exactly matches the tripod table presented here in Ill. 349. This table was formerly owned by W. P. Phillips, Montacute House, Somerset.

Among the published examples of tripod tables displaying the favored reverse shaping of tripod legs, as well as the crisply knuckled claws of the feet, but with less meticulous attention to the Dublin vine, foliage, and frill carving, is one Percy Macquoid drew attention to as typical of "Irish" work in his *Age of Mahogany,* Fig. 223. (Both features are seen in Ill. 350.) The table presented here is from Foster's Court Farm, near Gloucester, in the county adjoining Somerset.

A tripod table with spindle gallery, more heavily treated than the example in Ill. 355, and with characteristic satyr masks on the knees, was one of R. W. Symonds's favorite illustrations through which he unknowingly paid tribute to still another branch of Dublin furniture making. He repeatedly praised this tripod table for its "excellent design with appropriate and tasteful ornament and fine quality execution and material . . . an exceptionally well proportioned and graceful design, and . . . of the highest quality workmanship. The masks are typical both as regards design and execution of eighteenth century craftsmanship."

The tall post of Ill. 363 is from a bed in which the foreign wood of the rails, tester, and rear uprights might have proved unacceptable in an offering to a knowledgeable collector of Early American furniture. The typical paw foot and removable knee cap with spread eagle (adopted as an American emblem after 1790) are supplemented by Dublin vine carving and classic leaf collars. A close-up view of such a capping is given in Ill. 364. The carving of leafage and stippled ground effect on this example may be compared with a bedpost shown by Percy Macquoid (*Age of Mahogany,* Fig. 84). In Ill. 366, the separate capping appears in conjunction with an equally typical webbed claw-and-ball foot.

Although London designs were available in Dublin when the Duke of Beaufort furnished his Chinese bedroom at Badminton House, the open fretwork, vigorously modeled dragons, gilded metal finial ornament, and icicle-like frieze are all innovations of the Dublin artificer. His English counterpart would have spent *his* time modifying the often unworkable sketches of local designers. A final confirmation of this Dublin piece was found in the similarly treated uprights of the settee once owned by Governor Winthrop (Ill. 323) .

A separate volume could be devoted solely to the great number of urn stands and silver tables upon which Dublin artificers lavished their intricate woodworking skills and creative talents. Certain blind- and open-fret patterns were of course more popular than others in this particular field, and these appear often in other types of cabinetwork and seat furniture. For instance, an open-fret pattern used for the gallery of a silver table has been exactly repeated in the three-quarter gallery surmounting a desk of the form shown in Ill. 395.

In terms of the present study, these blind- and open-fret patterns, or even separate units where such bands, borders, and frieze panels are composed of a combination of these units, are of the utmost importance. This also applies to the treatment of legs and stretchers in seat furniture, cabinets-on-stands, and so on. A simplified version of the intricate stretcher in Ill. 377, with just one or two simple piercings in each arm (as in the outer portion of the stretcher shown in Ill. 386) , will link certain designs of silver tables to those of drop-leaf or pembroke tables, and to other pieces as well.

The highly skilled production of breakfast or tea tables, dressing tables, with open fretwork enclosing an undershelf, and worktables, such as the Badminton House example (*Georgian Cabinet-Makers,* Fig. 116) , apparently enabled Dublin cabinetmakers to rival Chippendale in the supply of homes not only in Gloucestershire, but in Worcestershire and Ayrshire as well. The example selected here (Ill. 388) also indicates the continued popularity of the triangular drop-leaf top surface, formerly supported on cabriole legs.

Another Dublin piece incorporating the same type of split-leg support as seen in Ill. 390 was illustrated by Percy Macquoid (*Age of Mahogany*, Fig. 237) as the property of Lord St. Oswald. It should be recognized that Lord St. Oswald was one of the nineteenth-century collectors of the very finest eighteenth-century Dublin furniture, and that his activity in this field and the name of Nostell Priory has resulted in the usual assignment of such pieces to English origin. A widespread lack of acquaintance with the high quality of such furniture is also obvious in a statement regarding some ribbon-back seat furniture (*op. cit.* Figs. 178 and 179, and *cf.* 175) Lord St. Oswald acquired "about 1883." The statement declared that the piece, being based on a *Director* design and "being of high quality, may reasonably be assigned to Chippendale" (*Georgian Cabinet-Makers*, 1955, p. 70).

Handles are very important adjuncts to many designs of Irish furniture, especially in tables and pedestal desks. In Irish homes today, pedestal desks of very simple design appear exactly as in Ill. 398. The only ornamentation of these pedestal desks are moldings and handles; occasionally, their plain ends may be relieved by an applied panel molding with incurvate corners.

Ill. 397 shows a continuation of the earlier Dublin designs in library or partner's desks of two sections that might be used separately as wall pieces or commodes. Typical of Dublin preference is the carving of the pilasters and pierced corner brackets, the blind-fret frieze band, and the ormolu handles indicating by their angularity a transition from late eighteenth- to early nineteenth-century work in this medium. These handles had been accepted at face value as original, but this had not been confirmed by further examination. Therefore, I wrote to a dealer with whom I had discussed his tremendous supplies of fine Irish furniture, obtained throughout recent decades from his private sources in that country, and into whose hands this particular desk had come after its sale by Parke-Bernet Galleries. My inquiry about the originality of these Dublin handles was entirely disregarded. Instead I was informed that "I am very sorry to say that I cannot agree with you that either this desk or many other items are Irish. No doubt there were good cabinet makers in Ireland, but practically all the well known (*sic!*) cabinet makers in the 18th century were from England. No doubt the Irish cabinet makers followed what was the English fashion, but considering that the population of Ireland in the 18th century was probably less than one tenth (*sic!*) of that of England I cannot consider it feasible that most of the furniture that we consider Chippendale, Haig, Vile, or Vile and Cobb, Mainwaring, Ince & Mayhew and numerous others really originated in Ireland. I would not like to accept the Irish attribution without definite proof." In view of this statement provided by the one authority best qualified above all others to distinguish (or not to distinguish) between Irish and English furniture, and in keeping with the formerly expressed suggestion of the term to cover all such possible and/or probable contingencies, this desk, as well as the preceding one, is shown here as "British." (If handles original: Dublin, eighteenth to nineteenth century.)

Another reliable way to label antique furniture of the British Isles appeared in the remarkably frank and accurate description given the pedestal desk in Ill. 399: "An exceptionally fine quality late 18th Century mahogany pedestal desk on ogee feet with serpentine front, back and sides, the canted corners with boxwood inlay and the leather line top bordered in satinwood." The general form of this piece appears in an earlier Dublin production with corbeled and richly carved stiles, and a more characteristic, rococo handle, in all respects a late Chippendale or transitional Chippendale-Hepplewhite design. In this instance, the contributor has shown an understanding of the time lapse that does occur in the production of some pieces where an earlier form has been retained and enhanced with later details of ornamentation.

Just as certain legs of silver tables were approximated in drop-leaf or pembroke tables, so those legs were repeated in card tables, sometimes along with their brackets. Where top and frieze shapings continued in parallel lines, they developed into the graceful serpentine curves of the table shown in Ill. 406. The top surfaces here are veneered either in padauk or one of the various rosewoods that appealed to Dublin cabinetmakers. Another very fine example of a similarly shaped card table, from the Earl of Leitrim, Mulroy, County Donegal, Ireland, may be seen by anyone fortunate enough to possess a copy of M. Harris's second catalogue of old English furniture. A Dublin table even finer than the one in Ill. 401 was illustrated in *Country Life* for November 25, 1924.

Some slight indication of the limitless variations that are possible in the forming of fret patterns may be seen by comparing the frieze bands in Ills. 408, 410, and 411. In Ill. 411, the carver may well have had access to an offering by Chippendale—a plate where another fret pattern is similar in outline to the plainer one used for the inside surfaces of the legs appearing in Ill. 416. Instead of recognizing the widespread availability of such patterns and details—in some instances through publications not confined to distribution in the British Isles but available throughout Europe—they are at times accepted as evidence of manufacture by the distributing designer and/or copyist, even where no such manufacture has been established.

From the number of consoles and side tables shown in published views of Irish interiors it is evident that Dublin carvers were especially partial to the use of separately treated reverse curves in fashioning the two or four supports of such tables as in Ill. 413. A simplified handling of this effect may be seen in the legs of a kettle stand illustrated by Percy Macquoid, *Age of Mahogany*, Fig. 226.

In the Chinese Chippendale side table (Ill. 419), the repeat pattern of the frieze is especially important as it is found—without the rosettes—in several outstanding kneehole cabinets of Chippendale and transitional Chippendale-Hepplewhite designs, and in kneehole writing tables (*Georgian Cabinet-Makers*, Fig. 103), which have erroneously been attributed to Chippendale. Another of these sideboard-tables (*Age of Mahogany*, Fig. 205), features additional fret treatments, brackets, and so on favored by Dublin artificers.

The heavily carved and sometimes inlaid serpentine or serpentine-bombé commodes, which R. W. Symonds has published as "Continental," but which are very florid Irish examples, nevertheless bring auction prices well up in the thousands of dollars. These are not the kinds of Dublin pieces I wish to popularize here. Satyr masks as stile capitals, along with lateral mounts, handles, and other ormolu work, distinguish the more acceptable inlaid commode seen in Plate 189, standing beside an equally typical Irish parcel-gilded side chair.

Handles, and even their bails and post plates, are very important in their original use on Dublin commodes. Those on the example in Ill. 422 are of the same pattern used for the library table previously mentioned as belonging to Sir Alfred Beit, one which is always worth considering as evidence of possible Dublin productions of tables, desks, chests of drawers, secretaires, and cabinets of various forms and sizes.

The dies and corbeled stiles of Ill. 423 appear in exactly the same conjunctive use on very important Dublin breakfront bookcases with cleft pediments, sometimes with lateral open-fret crest galleries of the pattern shown in Ill. 455. The underbodies of such pieces may also feature cupboard doors faced entirely with uninterrupted veneer surfaces.

There are numerous variations of the Dublin kneehole writing table as seen in Ill. 424. The canted and corbeled stiles of these pieces may be enriched with typical Dublin carving of blossoms, leafage, ribbons, and so on, or left plain beneath their leaf-carved corbels. R. W. Symonds has published an example of a pair with most characteristic Dublin handles, along with a leaf for use when they are placed back to back. A similar pair has been illustrated as the property of the Earl of Moray, Kinfauns Castle, Perthshire (Scotland). A somewhat similarly treated chest of drawers appears in the *Age of Mahogany*, Fig. 129, as the property of Viscount Enfield.

In its general form, the example shown in Ill. 429 appears in variations with different types of the most distinctive Dublin handles. One such piece, with *Chinese* feet, has been illustrated (*op. cit.* Fig. 135), and another appears in the *Dictionary of English Furniture*, Fig. 37.

Actually a precursor of Hepplewhite designs, the commode in Ill. 430 has the same type of frilled scrolls outlining its valanced lower drawer as appears in an illustrated example (*op. cit.* Pl. X) with ormolu stile capitals and hoof feet.

In Ill. 431 the handles are original and vary from those in Ill. 432, a pattern found in Dublin furniture of Hepplewhite designs. As a matter of fact, the latter piece, despite its fretted stiles and ogee bracket feet, was made around the turn of the century as evidenced by the use of grooved slips holding the bottom boards of its drawers.

Additional examples of the chest-on-chest, with fret patterns, feet, handles, and a typical square-sided, fall-front, elaborately treated writing drawer, all typical of Dublin furniture, are available in the *Dictionary of English Furniture*, Fig. 35, and Jourdain and Rose, Fig. 123.

By storing ornamental and structural details, the computer-like system I have developed has, through an examination of only the exposed features of a very plain bureau (Ill. 438), indicated an Irish provenance. In a reappearance of this piece its interior details provided the confirmatory evidence and indicated a relationship with American work of similar character. In the bureau (Ill. 436), the base should be compared with that of a secretaire (*Charles II— George II*, Fig. 210) with fret cresting.

The secretaire in Ill. 440 demonstrates the form adopted in American kettle-base furniture. To students of English furniture, however, the fret-carved central section of the writing interior should hold greater importance. This fret design is approximated on the cupboard doors of a kneehole writing table published as the property of the Honorable Mrs. Reginald Fellowes, while another such table (*Georgian Cabinet-Makers*, Fig. 103) is quite similarly treated; both feature the Dublin fret frieze bands that are so important in tracing such furniture.

More conventional fret carving appears in a secretaire (*op. cit.* 64), presenting all typical Dublin features including most distinctive brasses (see also Cescinsky, p. 270). A cresting of Prince of Wales plumes has been considered evidence that this piece was "Probably made for George, Prince of Wales (later George III) by William Vile." The favorite Prince of Wales plumes of Dublin carvers is missing in a similar piece, published in an M. Harris catalogue as owned by Princess Hatzfeldt, Foliejon Park, Winkfield, near Windsor, in which only the shape of the bracket feet differ.

An astragal pattern similar to that in Ill. 442 appears in a secretaire (*Age of Mahogany*, Fig. 146), in which the doors close in the characteristic Dublin overlap, as seen (*op. cit.* Fig. 236) in Ills. 453 and 454, and in Jourdain and Rose, Fig. 99.

The more important examples of Chinese Chippendale furniture will bear comparison with the bureau-cabinet "with perforated pagoda roof" illustrated in the *Dictionary of English Furniture,* in which the Chinese foot resembles that of the dressing chest (*Age of Mahogany,* Fig. 135) owned by Lord St. Oswald.

Characteristic Dublin carving is featured in the tea caddy (Ill. 449), and various fret patterns appear in Ills. 450–452. In Ill. 452, the circa date would be nearer to 1800 than 1760, indicating a time lapse in production. While an eighteenth-century date was obvious in examining the cabinet of Ill. 453, the one in Ill. 454, which has not been examined, has been labeled circa 1840, apparently through the general misunderstanding that to be genuinely antique a piece cannot be of an age less than its design indicates in relation to English developments. The museum was good enough to send two screws from the door hinges for examination. These were found to be made by hand, probably before 1817, the earliest date associated with the invention of the thread-cutting machine.

In its general form, the writing cabinet in Ill. 455 was continued in transitional Chippendale-Hepplewhite and Adam-Hepplewhite designs. From the standpoint of these researches, the most important feature of all is the fret pattern appearing in the front and side frieze bands of the wing sections. This same fret frieze is a feature of numerous Dublin bookcases with cleft or scrolled pediments or straight tops, featuring smooth veneers combined with corbeled stiles, as in Ill. 423. Later, the veneers were inlaid with panel bandings and interlaced foliations at their incurvate corners.

Cabinet-secretaires, similar in form to a "Dressing Chest and Bookcase" published in the 1754 edition of Chippendale's *Director,* were produced in variations with typical Dublin treatments in applied carving, fret bands, galleries, and so on, and continued in favor with an adoption of Gothic astragals and spires (see Ill. 462) and oval mirror panels enclosed by classic drapery or husk festoons.

Another long continued favorite of Dublin cabinetmakers, which was apparently still being supplied to Scotland and elsewhere in Great Britain during the early years of the nineteenth century, was the breakfront bookcase with pagoda-form median molding and shaped panel moldings with four so-called Vile and Cobb leaf clasps. One representative example (*Age of Mahogany,* Pl. XV) is surmounted by a pagoda roof; another (Jourdain and Rose, Fig. 83) by a cleft pediment; and a third (Cescinsky, p. 279) has a fret band at the base of a pattern linking it to a different design (*Age of Mahogany,* Fig. 148), and is owned by the Duke of Beaufort, Badminton House, Gloucestershire. This latter example is important for its various fret patterns, beveled door panels, and a favorite Irish use of wire-mesh screening in its lateral doors.

Bookcases of the Chippendale design shown in Ill. 461 generally appear in Irish and Scottish collections of long standing. One similar in most respects but without a cleft pediment was illustrated in the *Connoisseur,* February, 1939, p. xi, as having been made for the Bishop of Armagh. Others follow the same lines but may be overenriched with the coarser type of Irish foliage carving. The design is *said* to have been transferred to America between 1760 and 1770 by Thomas Elfe of Charleston.

Spire finials, in many variations of those surmounting the pedimented fret gallery of Ill. 402, are key items that should attract attention in all further investigations into the finest Dublin cabinet pieces. The blind and pierced fret patterns and that of the astragals are typical, while the original ormolu mounts of the drawers represent work in this medium that has often been described as the very finest ever to be produced by the most highly skilled of English metalists. In connection with Ill. 414, featuring typical interrupted scrolls in its pediment, comparison should be made with an example (Ellwood, Fig. 89) in which the lower door panels are handled in the same manner as those of the Badminton House bookcase (*Age of Mahogany,* Fig. 148). Another (*op. cit.* 149) displays a wealth of typical ornamental and structural features. This last example of Dublin furniture presented here is certainly worthy of acknowledgment since it reflects the selective taste of Daniel Farr, the man responsible for having brought to this country so many of the pieces represented in these illustrations.

Acknowledgment is also made of two items uncovered through an investigation sponsored by R. W. Symonds in an attempt to discover whether English furniture ever arrived in Ireland during the eighteenth century. While no such record was found, the *Dublin Journal* of August 29, 1747, advertised a "great Choice of Guilt Leather and painted Screens." From examples shown in Irish interiors that resemble the one shown in Ill. 465—with the same nailed gilt-edging strips—it is apparent that this may well be one of these advertised screens.

The second item, appearing in the *Dublin Journal* of November 24, 1747, offered "great Quantities of India Paper for Screens or Hangings," and drew attention to the skill of "Michael Spruson" in applying these papers to walls and screens. Spruson was highly recommended by the ladies he had pleased for "improving and amending, such as has been ill done, by the Unskilful." Ill. 466 shows a set of such Chinese painted paper panels, of about that date, ready for dismantling, which would be a difficult undertaking if originally "ill done" by not being properly laid on canvas.

PLATES

PLATE 1

1. QUEEN ANNE CARVED, PARCEL-GILDED, AND DECORATED RED LACQUER SIDE CHAIR

2. QUEEN ANNE DECORATED BLACK AND GOLD LACQUER SIDE CHAIR

3. QUEEN ANNE WALNUT TALL-BACK UPHOLSTERED CHAIR

4. QUEEN ANNE WALNUT TALL-BACK UPHOLSTERED SIDE CHAIR IN NEEDLEWORK

PLATE 2

5. QUEEN ANNE WALNUT UPHOLSTERED
ARMCHAIR IN NEEDLEWORK

6. QUEEN ANNE WALNUT UPHOLSTERED
ARMCHAIR

7. QUEEN ANNE WALNUT UPHOLSTERED
ARMCHAIR

8. QUEEN ANNE WALNUT UPHOLSTERED
ARMCHAIR

PLATE 3

9. QUEEN ANNE WALNUT ARMCHAIR

10. QUEEN ANNE CARVED WALNUT
SIDE CHAIR

11. QUEEN ANNE WALNUT SIDE CHAIR

12. QUEEN ANNE CARVED WALNUT SIDE
CHAIR

PLATE 4

13. QUEEN ANNE CARVED WALNUT AND
MARQUETRY SIDE CHAIR

14. QUEEN ANNE WALNUT MARQUETRY
SIDE CHAIR

15. QUEEN ANNE INLAID WALNUT
ARMCHAIR

16. QUEEN ANNE DECORATED RED
LACQUER SIDE CHAIR
*Victoria and Albert Museum Crown
Copyright*

PLATE 5

17. QUEEN ANNE WALNUT TWO-CHAIR-BACK SETTEE

18. QUEEN ANNE WALNUT DAYBED

PLATE 6

19. QUEEN ANNE WALNUT AND MARQUETRY
SIDE CHAIR WITH CIPHER OF DUDLEY NORTH
*Victoria and Albert Museum Crown
Copyright*

20. QUEEN ANNE INLAID WALNUT AND
MARQUETRY UPHOLSTERED SIDE CHAIR

21. QUEEN ANNE SILVER GESSO
UPHOLSTERED SIDE CHAIR
Courtesy of Temple Williams Ltd., London

22. QUEEN ANNE CARVED WALNUT AND
MARQUETRY SIDE CHAIR
*Courtesy of French & Co., Inc., New
York City*

PLATE 7

23. QUEEN ANNE CARVED WALNUT SIDE
CHAIR
*Courtesy of Mallett & Son (Antiques)
Ltd., London*

24. QUEEN ANNE CARVED WALNUT AND
MARQUETRY ARMCHAIR
*Courtesy of French & Co., Inc., New
York City*

25. QUEEN ANNE CARVED WALNUT TWO-CHAIR-BACK SETTEE

PLATE 8

26. QUEEN ANNE CARVED WALNUT TWO-CHAIR-BACK SETTEE
Courtesy of Needham's Antiques Inc., New York City

27. EARLY GEORGIAN CARVED WALNUT
SIDE CHAIR
Sold at $425 by Parke-Bernet Galleries,
Inc., New York City

28. EARLY GEORGIAN CARVED MAHOGANY
ARMCHAIR

PLATE 9

29. EARLY GEORGIAN CARVED WALNUT SIDE CHAIR

30. EARLY GEORGIAN CARVED WALNUT SIDE CHAIR

31. QUEEN ANNE CARVED UPHOLSTERED DRUNKARD'S CHAIR

PLATE 10

32. QUEEN ANNE CARVED WALNUT WING CHAIR

33. QUEEN ANNE CARVED WALNUT WING CHAIR

PLATE 11

34. QUEEN ANNE CARVED WALNUT WING CHAIR

35. QUEEN ANNE CARVED WALNUT WING CHAIR
Sold at $2,100 by Parke-Bernet Galleries,
Inc., New York City

PLATE 12

36. QUEEN ANNE WALNUT SPOON-BACK
WRITING CHAIR
Sold at $1,000 by Parke-Bernet
Galleries, Inc., New York City

37. EARLY GEORGIAN CARVED WALNUT
SIDE CHAIR

38. EARLY GEORGIAN MAHOGANY
STRADDLE CHAIR

39. EARLY GEORGIAN MAHOGANY
UPHOLSTERED ARMCHAIR

PLATE 13

40. EARLY GEORGIAN CARVED WALNUT
ARMCHAIR
*Courtesy of Mallett & Son (Antiques)
Ltd., London*

41. EARLY GEORGIAN CARVED WALNUT
WING CHAIR

42. EARLY GEORGIAN CARVED MAHOGANY TWO-CHAIR-BACK SETTEE
Victoria and Albert Museum Crown Copyright

PLATE 14

43. EARLY GEORGIAN CARVED WALNUT SPOON-BACK
WRITING CHAIR

44. EARLY GEORGIAN CARVED WALNUT SPOON-BACK
WRITING CHAIR
Sold at $3,100 by Parke-Bernet Galleries, Inc.,
New York City

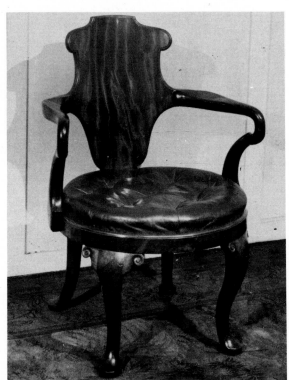

45. EARLY GEORGIAN MAHOGANY SPOON-BACK
WRITING CHAIR
*Courtesy of Needham's Antiques, Inc., New
York City*

46. EARLY GEORGIAN CARVED MAHOGANY SPOON-
BACK WRITING CHAIR

PLATE 15

47. EARLY GEORGIAN CARVED WALNUT
ARMCHAIR

48. EARLY GEORGIAN CARVED WALNUT
SIDE CHAIR

49. EARLY GEORGIAN CARVED WALNUT
SIDE CHAIR
Sold at $1,600 a pair, by Parke-Bernet
Galleries, Inc., New York City

50. EARLY GEORGIAN CARVED WALNUT
ARMCHAIR
(The front rail poorly restored)

PLATE 16

51. EARLY GEORGIAN CARVED WALNUT
SHEPHERD'S-CROOK ARMCHAIR
Sold at $2,700 by Parke-Bernet
Galleries, Inc., New York City

52. EARLY GEORGIAN CARVED WALNUT
SIDE CHAIR
Sold at $1,000 a pair by Parke-Bernet
Galleries, Inc., New York City

53. EARLY GEORGIAN CARVED WALNUT
SIDE CHAIR
Sold at $800 a pair by Parke-Bernet
Galleries, Inc., New York City

54. EARLY GEORGIAN CARVED WALNUT
AND MARQUETRY ARMCHAIR
*Victoria and Albert Museum Crown
Copyright*

PLATE 17

55. EARLY GEORGIAN CARVED WALNUT
SHEPHERD'S-CROOK ARMCHAIR

56. EARLY GEORGIAN WALNUT SIDE
CHAIR

57. EARLY GEORGIAN CARVED
MAHOGANY SIDE CHAIR

58. EARLY GEORGIAN CARVED
MAHOGANY ARMCHAIR

PLATE 18

59. EARLY GEORGIAN CARVED MAHOGANY SIDE CHAIR

60. EARLY GEORGIAN CARVED MAHOGANY SIDE CHAIR

61. EARLY GEORGIAN CARVED WALNUT ARMCHAIR

62. EARLY GEORGIAN CARVED WALNUT SIDE CHAIR
Sold at $1,200 a pair by Parke-Bernet Galleries, Inc., New York City

PLATE 19

63. EARLY GEORGIAN CARVED
MAHOGANY SIDE CHAIR
Sold at $375 by Parke-Bernet
Galleries, Inc., New York City

64. EARLY GEORGIAN CARVED AND
PARCEL-GILDED ARMORIAL SIDE CHAIR
*Courtesy of the Cooper Union
Museum, New York City*

65. EARLY GEORGIAN CARVED AND
GILDED ARMORIAL SIDE CHAIR
*Victoria and Albert Museum Crown
Copyright*

66. EARLY GEORGIAN CARVED WALNUT
ARMCHAIR
Sold at $2,900 by Parke-Bernet
Galleries, Inc., New York City

PLATE 20

67. EARLY GEORGIAN CARVED WALNUT TWO-CHAIR-BACK SETTEE
Courtesy of J. J. Wolff (Antiques) Ltd., New York City

68. EARLY GEORGIAN CARVED WALNUT TWO-CHAIR-BACK SETTEE
Sold at $900 by Parke-Bernet Galleries, Inc., New York City

PLATE 21

69. EARLY GEORGIAN CARVED WALNUT AND MAHOGANY
ARMCHAIR
Sold at $800 by Parke-Bernet Galleries, Inc.,
New York City

70. EARLY GEORGIAN CARVED
MAHOGANY SIDE CHAIR

71. EARLY GEORGIAN CARVED VIRGINIA
AND EUROPEAN WALNUT SIDE CHAIR
Sold at $650 a pair by Parke-Bernet
Galleries, Inc., New York City

PLATE 22

72. EARLY GEORGIAN CARVED MAHOGANY
UPHOLSTERED ARMCHAIR

73. EARLY GEORGIAN CARVED MAHOGANY
UPHOLSTERED SIDE CHAIR

74. EARLY GEORGIAN CARVED MAHOGANY UPHOLSTERED SETTEE

PLATE 23

75. EARLY GEORGIAN CARVED MAHOGANY
SIDE CHAIR
Sold at $750 by Parke-Bernet
Galleries, Inc., New York City

76. EARLY GEORGIAN CARVED MAHOGANY
ARMCHAIR

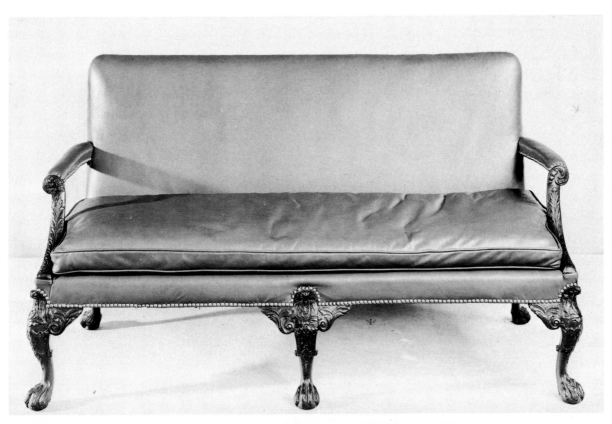

77. EARLY GEORGIAN CARVED PADAUK UPHOLSTERED SETTEE

PLATE 24

78. EARLY GEORGIAN CARVED WALNUT OPEN-ARM EASY CHAIR
Sold at $1,075 by Parke-Bernet Galleries, Inc., New York City

79. EARLY GEORGIAN CARVED BLACK WALNUT OPEN-ARM EASY CHAIR

80. EARLY GEORGIAN CARVED MAHOGANY OPEN-ARM SETTEE

PLATE 25

81. EARLY GEORGIAN CARVED MAHOGANY
UPHOLSTERED SIDE CHAIR IN ORIGINAL NEEDLEWORK
Courtesy of The Leicester Museum

PLATE 26

82. DETAIL OF THE LEG OF 81.

83. EARLY GEORGIAN CARVED MAHOGANY ARMCHAIR
Sold at $2,000 a pair by Parke-Bernet Galleries, Inc., New York City

84. EARLY GEORGIAN CARVED MAHOGANY SIDE CHAIR

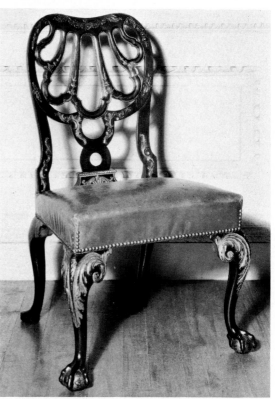

85. EARLY GEORGIAN CARVED AND PARCEL-GILDED MAHOGANY SIDE CHAIR
Courtesy of the Philadelphia Museum of Art

PLATE 27

86. GEORGIAN CARVED MAHOGANY STOOL WITH DOLPHIN FEET
Victoria and Albert Museum Crown Copyright

87. GEORGIAN CARVED MAHOGANY
WHEELBACK ARMCHAIR WITH DOLPHIN FEET

88. EARLY GEORGIAN CARVED MAHOGANY
UPHOLSTERED ARMCHAIR
Sold at $850 by Parke-Bernet Galleries, Inc.,
New York City

89. EARLY GEORGIAN CARVED WALNUT UPHOLSTERED
ARMCHAIR
Victoria and Albert Museum Crown Copyright

PLATE 28

90. EARLY GEORGIAN CARVED MAHOGANY TWO-BACK SETTEE
Sold at $1,700 by Parke-Bernet Galleries, Inc., New York City

91. EARLY GEORGIAN CARVED MAHOGANY UPHOLSTERED SETTEE
Courtesy of French & Co., Inc., New York City

PLATE 29

92. EARLY GEORGIAN CARVED MAHOGANY
SIDE CHAIR
Sold at $500 by Parke-Bernet Galleries,
Inc., New York City

93. EARLY GEORGIAN CARVED WALNUT
AND ASH SIDE CHAIR

94. EARLY GEORGIAN CARVED MAHOGANY
SIDE CHAIR
*Victoria and Albert Museum Crown
Copyright*

95. EARLY GEORGIAN CARVED MAHOGANY
SIDE CHAIR

PLATE 30

96. EARLY GEORGIAN MAHOGANY STRADDLE CHAIR

97. EARLY GEORGIAN CARVED MAHOGANY STRADDLE CHAIR

98. EARLY GEORGIAN CARVED BEECH CORNER CHAIR

99. EARLY GEORGIAN CARVED WALNUT CORNER CHAIR
Victoria and Albert Museum Crown Copyright

PLATE 31

100. EARLY GEORGIAN CARVED WALNUT
LADY'S WING CHAIR
Sold at $725 by Parke-Bernet
Galleries, Inc., New York City

101. EARLY GEORGIAN SHELL-CARVED
ARMCHAIR WITH SHAPED STRETCHER

102. EARLY GEORGIAN CARVED WALNUT
SIDE CHAIR

103. EARLY GEORGIAN CARVED WALNUT
SMALL WING CHAIR
Sold at $850 by Parke-Bernet
Galleries, Inc., New York City

PLATE 32

104. EARLY GEORGIAN CARVED WALNUT
SIDE CHAIR

105. EARLY GEORGIAN WALNUT ARMCHAIR

106. EARLY GEORGIAN CARVED WALNUT
SIDE CHAIR

107. EARLY GEORGIAN CARVED WALNUT
SIDE CHAIR

PLATE 33

108. EARLY GEORGIAN CARVED MAHOGANY
SIDE CHAIR

109. EARLY GEORGIAN CARVED MAHOGANY
SIDE CHAIR

110. EARLY GEORGIAN CARVED MAHOGANY
SIDE CHAIR

111. EARLY GEORGIAN CARVED WALNUT
SIDE CHAIR

PLATE 34

112. EARLY GEORGIAN CARVED MAHOGANY
TASSEL-BACK SIDE CHAIR

113. EARLY GEORGIAN CARVED MAHOGANY
TASSEL-BACK SIDE CHAIR

114. EARLY GEORGIAN CARVED WALNUT
TASSEL-BACK SIDE CHAIR

115. EARLY GEORGIAN TASSEL-BACK
ARMCHAIR WITH TURNED LEGS

PLATE 35

116. EARLY GEORGIAN CARVED MAHOGANY TWO-CHAIR-BACK SETTEE

117. EARLY GEORGIAN CARVED WALNUT
ARMCHAIR
Sold at $1,050 by Parke-Bernet
Galleries, Inc., New York City

118. EARLY GEORGIAN CARVED WALNUT
SIDE CHAIR

PLATE 36

119. EARLY GEORGIAN CARVED WALNUT
ARMCHAIR WITH EAGLE-HEAD ARM TERMINALS

120. EARLY GEORGIAN CARVED MAHOGANY SIDE
CHAIR
Sold at $550 each by Parke-Bernet
Galleries, Inc., New York City

121. EARLY GEORGIAN CARVED MAHOGANY
ARMCHAIR

122. EARLY GEORGIAN CARVED WALNUT ARMCHAIR

PLATE 37

123. EARLY GEORGIAN CARVED MAHOGANY
UPHOLSTERED OPEN-ARM EASY CHAIR

124. EARLY GEORGIAN CARVED MAHOGANY
UPHOLSTERED OPEN-ARM EASY CHAIR

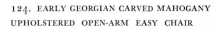

125. EARLY GEORGIAN CARVED MAHOGANY
UPHOLSTERED OPEN-ARM EASY CHAIR

126. EARLY GEORGIAN CARVED MAHOGANY
UPHOLSTERED OPEN-ARM EASY CHAIR

PLATE 38

127. EARLY GEORGIAN CARVED MAHOGANY
WING CHAIR

128. EARLY GEORGIAN CARVED WALNUT WING
CHAIR

PLATE 39

129. QUEEN ANNE YEWWOOD BURL AND WALNUT SIDE TABLE
Courtesy of Biggs of Maidenhead Ltd.

PLATE 40

130. QUEEN ANNE INLAID WALNUT SIDE TABLE

131. QUEEN ANNE INLAID WALNUT SIDE TABLE
Sold at $725 by Parke-Bernet Galleries, Inc.,
New York City

132. QUEEN ANNE INLAID WALNUT SIDE TABLE

133. QUEEN ANNE CARVED AND INLAID WALNUT SIDE
TABLE

PLATE 41

134. QUEEN ANNE SEMIELLIPTICAL CARD TABLE WITH BALUSTER LEGS AND FLAT CUSPED STRETCHER
Courtesy of Mallett & Son (Antiques) Ltd., London

PLATE 42

135. QUEEN ANNE CARVED AND INLAID
WALNUT SEMIELLIPTICAL CARD TABLE
Sold at $3,400 by Parke-Bernet
Galleries, Inc., New York City

136. QUEEN ANNE CARVED AND INLAID
WALNUT SERPENTINE CARD TABLE WITH
NEEDLEWORK SURFACE
Sold at $2,900 by Parke-Bernet
Galleries, Inc., New York City

PLATE 43

137. QUEEN ANNE WALNUT SIDE TABLE WITH HOOF FEET

138. WILLIAM AND MARY INLAID WALNUT AND SPIRAL-TURNED
ASH SIDE TABLE

PLATE 44

139. WILLIAM AND MARY WALNUT OYSTERWOOD AND MARQUETRY FALL-FRONT WRITING CABINET-ON-STAND

PLATE 45

140. WILLIAM AND MARY WALNUT OYSTERWOOD AND MARQUETRY FALL-FRONT WRITING CABINET-ON-STAND

PLATE 46

141. WILLIAM AND MARY OYSTER PARQUETRY FALL-FRONT WRITING CABINET-ON-STAND
Courtesy of Hotspur Ltd., London

PLATE 47

142. QUEEN ANNE INLAID BURL WALNUT CHEST-ON-STAND

PLATE 48

143. LATE QUEEN ANNE CARVED AND INLAID WALNUT DRESSING BUREAU

PLATE 49

144. QUEEN ANNE INLAID WALNUT
BUREAU WITH BALUSTER LEGS
*Courtesy of The Montreal Museum of
Fine Arts*

145. QUEEN ANNE CARVED AND INLAID
WALNUT BUREAU-ON-STAND
Sold at £945 by Christie, Manson &
Woods, London

PLATE 50

146. QUEEN ANNE INLAID WALNUT AND OYSTERWOOD PARQUETRY FALL-FRONT WRITING CABINET-ON-STAND

PLATE 51

148. QUEEN ANNE INLAID WALNUT BUREAU

147. QUEEN ANNE INLAID WALNUT
PEDESTAL DESK
Sold at $3,100 by Parke-Bernet
Galleries, Inc., New York City

PLATE 52

149. QUEEN ANNE INLAID BURL WALNUT SECRETAIRE
Courtesy of French & Company, Inc., New York City

PLATE 53

150. QUEEN ANNE INLAID BURL WALNUT SECRETAIRE
Courtesy of French & Company, Inc., New York City

PLATE 54

151. QUEEN ANNE INLAID WALNUT SECRETAIRE

PLATE 55

152. QUEEN ANNE INLAID WALNUT SECRETAIRE

153. QUEEN ANNE INLAID WALNUT SECRETAIRE

PLATE 56

154. QUEEN ANNE INLAID WALNUT AND BURL WALNUT SECRETAIRE
Courtesy of the Nordiska Museet, Stockholm

PLATE 57

155. QUEEN ANNE INLAID WALNUT SECRETAIRE
Sold at $2,300 by Parke-Bernet Galleries, Inc., New York City

PLATE 58

156. QUEEN ANNE INLAID WALNUT
KNEEHOLE WRITING OR DRESSING TABLE
Sold at $550 by Parke-Bernet
Galleries, Inc., New York City

157. QUEEN ANNE INLAID WALNUT
KNEEHOLE WRITING OR DRESSING TABLE

PLATE 59

158. QUEEN ANNE INLAID WALNUT
CHEST OF DRAWERS
Sold at $550 by Parke-Bernet
Galleries, Inc., New York City

159. QUEEN ANNE WALNUT MARQUETRY
CHEST OF DRAWERS

PLATE 60

160. QUEEN ANNE INLAID WALNUT CHEST-ON-CHEST
Victoria and Albert Museum Crown Copyright

PLATE 61

161. QUEEN ANNE INLAID WALNUT BOOKCASE
Courtesy of Biggs of Maidenhead Ltd.

PLATE 62

162. QUEEN ANNE INLAID WALNUT BOOKCASE
Courtesy of Biggs of Maidenhead Ltd.

PLATE 63

163. QUEEN ANNE WALNUT CABINET

PLATE 64

164. EARLY GEORGIAN MAHOGANY DRINKING
STAND
Courtesy of J. J. Wolff (Antiques) Ltd.,
New York City

165. EARLY GEORGIAN FRET-PIERCED MAHOGANY
BEDSIDE STAND
Sold at $450 by Parke-Bernet Galleries,
Inc., New York City

166. EARLY GEORGIAN MAHOGANY OCCASIONAL
TABLE

167. EARLY GEORGIAN CARVED MAHOGANY
TRIANGULAR DROP-LEAF TABLE

PLATE 65

168. EARLY GEORGIAN INLAID MAHOGANY
CENTER TABLE
Courtesy of Biggs of Maidenhead Ltd.

69. EARLY GEORGIAN CARVED PADAUK
RAY-TOP TABLE
ourtesy of Biggs of Maidenhead Ltd.

PLATE 66

170. EARLY GEORGIAN CARVED MAHOGANY
TRAY-TOP TABLE

171. EARLY GEORGIAN CARVED WALNUT
AND OYSTER PARQUETRY CENTER TABLE

PLATE 67

172. EARLY GEORGIAN CARVED MAHOGANY LIBRARY COMMODE WITH FOLDING TOP

173. EARLY GEORGIAN CARVED MAHOGANY LIBRARY TABLE
Victoria and Albert Museum Crown Copyright

PLATE 68

174. EARLY GEORGIAN CARVED MAHOGANY DROP-LEAF DINING TABLE
Sold at $1,500 by Parke-Bernet Galleries, Inc., New York City

175. EARLY GEORGIAN CARVED MAHOGANY DROP-LEAF SECTIONAL DINING TABLE
Sold at $3,200 by Parke-Bernet Galleries, Inc., New York City

PLATE 69

176. EARLY GEORGIAN MAHOGANY DROP-
LEAF DINING TABLE WITH HOOF FEET

177. EARLY GEORGIAN CARVED WALNUT
SIDE TABLE
Sold at $620 by Parke-Bernet
Galleries, Inc., New York City

PLATE 70

178. EARLY GEORGIAN CARVED
MAHOGANY SEMICIRCULAR CARD TABLE

179. EARLY GEORGIAN CARVED
MAHOGANY SEMICIRCULAR CARD TABLE

PLATE 71

180. EARLY GEORGIAN CARVED AND
INLAID WALNUT CARD TABLE
Sold at $1,050 by Parke-Bernet
Galleries, Inc., New York City

181. EARLY GEORGIAN CARVED AND
INLAID WALNUT CARD TABLE
Courtesy of Biggs of Maidenhead, Ltd.

PLATE 72

182. EARLY GEORGIAN CARVED AND
INLAID WALNUT CARD TABLE

183. EARLY GEORGIAN CARVED WALNUT
CARD TABLE

PLATE 73

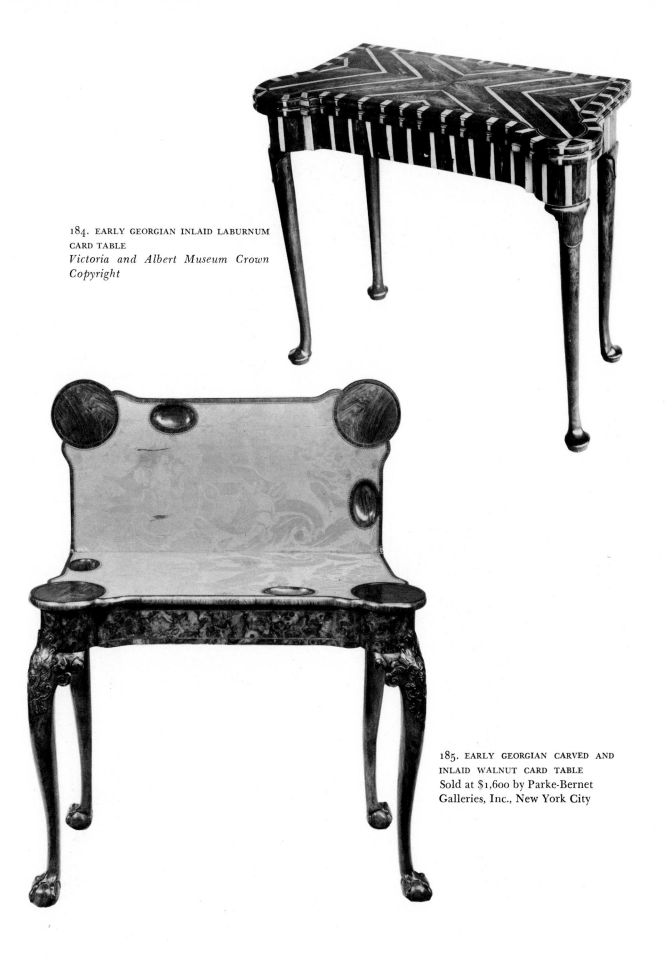

184. EARLY GEORGIAN INLAID LABURNUM
CARD TABLE
*Victoria and Albert Museum Crown
Copyright*

185. EARLY GEORGIAN CARVED AND
INLAID WALNUT CARD TABLE
Sold at $1,600 by Parke-Bernet
Galleries, Inc., New York City

PLATE 74

186. EARLY GEORGIAN CARVED
AND INLAID MAHOGANY CARD
TABLE

187. "PHILADELPHIA" CARVED
MAHOGANY CARD TABLE

PLATE 75

188. EARLY GEORGIAN CARVED MAHOGANY SIDE TABLE

189. EARLY GEORGIAN CARVED MAHOGANY SIDE TABLE

PLATE 76

190. EARLY GEORGIAN CARVED MAHOGANY SIDE TABLE
Sold at $1,800 by Parke-Bernet Galleries, Inc., New York City

PLATE 77

191. EARLY GEORGIAN CARVED MAHOGANY SIDE TABLE
Courtesy of French & Co., Inc., New York City

192. EARLY GEORGIAN CARVED MAHOGANY SIDE TABLE

PLATE 78

193. EARLY GEORGIAN CARVED MAHOGANY SIDE TABLE

194. EARLY GEORGIAN CARVED MAHOGANY SIDE TABLE

PLATE 79

195. QUEEN ANNE GILDED GESSO SIDE TABLE
*Courtesy of Mallett & Son (Antiques)
Ltd., London*

196. QUEEN ANNE GILDED GESSO SIDE TABLE
*Courtesy of Mallett & Son (Antiques)
Ltd., London*

PLATE 80

197. EARLY GEORGIAN GILDED GESSO
SIDE TABLE

198. GEORGIAN CARVED AND GILDED
CONSOLE TABLE

PLATE 81

199. EARLY GEORGIAN CARVED AND GILDED CONSOLE TABLE
Courtesy of Jeremy Ltd., London

PLATE 82

200. GEORGIAN CARVED AND GILDED EAGLE CONSOLE
Courtesy of Charles Lamb and Sons Ltd., Harrowgate

201. GEORGIAN CARVED AND GILDED EAGLE CONSOLE TABLE
Collection of the Earl of Carnarvon, Highclerc Castle, Newbury, Hants
Sold at $4,200 a pair by Parke-Bernet Galleries, Inc., New York City

PLATE 83

202. GEORGIAN CARVED AND GILDED EAGLE CONSOLE TABLE

PLATE 84

203. EARLY GEORGIAN INLAID YEW-WOOD-BURL KNEEHOLE DRESSING TABLE

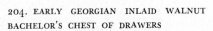

204. EARLY GEORGIAN INLAID WALNUT BACHELOR'S CHEST OF DRAWERS

PLATE 85

205. EARLY GEORGIAN DECORATED LACQUER BLOCKFRONT CHEST-ON-CHEST
Courtesy of Shreve, Crump & Low Company, Boston

PLATE 86

206. EARLY GEORGIAN INLAID WALNUT CHEST-ON-CHEST

PLATE 87

207. GEORGIAN INLAID WALNUT
BUREAU-ON-STAND

207A. EARLY GEORGIAN INLAID ASH
CHILD'S BLOCKFRONT BUREAU

PLATE 88

208. EARLY GEORGIAN INLAID
WALNUT KNEEHOLE BUREAU

209. EARLY GEORGIAN INLAID
WALNUT BUREAU

PLATE 89

210. EARLY GEORGIAN INLAID WALNUT SECRETAIRE WITH GLASS FINIALS
Courtesy of Christie, Manson & Woods, London

PLATE 90

211. EARLY GEORGIAN INLAID WALNUT SECRETAIRE

PLATE 91

212. EARLY GEORGIAN CARVED, INLAID, AND PARCEL-GILDED WALNUT SECRETAIRE

PLATE 92

213. SECTIONAL VIEW, INTERIOR OF EXAMPLE SHOWN IN ILL. 212

PLATE 93

214. SECTIONAL VIEW, INTERIOR OF EXAMPLE SHOWN IN ILL. 212

PLATE 94

215. EARLY GEORGIAN CARVED, INLAID, AND PARCEL-GILDED WALNUT SECRETAIRE
Sold at $2,000 by Parke-Bernet Galleries, Inc., New York City

PLATE 95

216. EARLY GEORGIAN CARVED MAHOGANY ARCHITECTURAL BUREAU-CABINET
Victoria and Albert Museum Crown Copyright

PLATE 96

217. EARLY GEORGIAN KINGWOOD PARQUETRY CABINET ON CARVED MAHOGANY STAND

PLATE 97

218. EARLY GEORGIAN CARVED MAHOGANY COLLECTOR'S CABINET
Courtesy of the Leeds City Art Galleries

PLATE 98

219. EARLY GEORGIAN CARVED MAHOGANY BOOKCASE

PLATE 99

220. EARLY GEORGIAN CARVED MAHOGANY BOOKCASE
Victoria and Albert Museum Crown Copyright

PLATE 100

221. EARLY GEORGIAN CARVED MAHOGANY BUREAU-CABINET
Courtesy of the Leeds City Art Galleries

PLATE 101

222. EARLY GEORGIAN CARVED MAHOGANY BOOKCASE
From Rokeby Hall, Yorkshire

PLATE 102

223. EARLY GEORGIAN MAHOGANY BUREAU BOOKCASE

PLATE 103

224. GEORGIAN CARVED MAHOGANY ARCHITECTURAL CABINET

PLATE 104

225. GEORGIAN CARVED MAHOGANY ARCHITECTURAL CABINET

PLATE 105

226. CHINESE DECORATED LACQUER CABINET ON CARVED AND GILDED STAND
Courtesy of Mallett & Son (Antiques) Ltd., London

PLATE 106

227. GEORGIAN DECORATED LACQUER CABINET ON CARVED AND GILDED STAND

PLATE 107

228. GEORGIAN DECORATED LACQUER CABINET ON CARVED AND GILDED STAND
Courtesy of Mallett & Son (Antiques) Ltd., London

229. GALLERY VIEW, BADMINTON HOUSE COMMODE-CABINET
Victoria and Albert Museum Crown Copyright

PLATE 108

230. GEORGIAN MAPLE KNURLWOOD CABINET ON CARVED AND GILDED STAND

PLATE 109

231. GEORGIAN DECORATED LACQUER CABINET ON CARVED AND GILDED STAND
Victoria and Albert Museum Crown Copyright

PLATE 110

232. GEORGIAN DECORATED LACQUER CABINET ON CARVED AND GILDED STAND
Courtesy of Mallett & Son (Antiques) Ltd., London

PLATE 111

233. GEORGIAN DECORATED LACQUER CABINET ON CARVED AND GILDED STAND
Courtesy of Mallett & Son (Antiques) Ltd., London

PLATE 112

234. CHIPPENDALE CARVED AND
DECORATED LACQUER TRIPOD TABLE
*Victoria and Albert Museum Crown
Copyright*

235. QUEEN ANNE DECORATED LACQUER
SIDE TABLE
*Courtesy of French & Co., Inc., New
York City*

PLATE 113

236. WILLIAM AND MARY PAINTED AND
DECORATED BUREAU-CABINET
Courtesy of Biggs of Maidenhead Ltd.

PLATE 114

237. EARLY GEORGIAN DECORATED LACQUER CABINET ON
GILDED GESSO STAND
*Courtesy of William Rockhill Nelson Gallery of Art
(Nelson Fund), Kansas City, Missouri*

PLATE 115

238. EARLY GEORGIAN DECORATED LACQUER CABINET ON GILDED GESSO STAND
*Courtesy of William Rockhill Nelson Gallery of Art (Nelson Fund),
Kansas City, Missouri*

PLATE 116

239. QUEEN ANNE DECORATED LACQUER SECRETAIRE

PLATE 117

240. EARLY GEORGIAN DECORATED LACQUER BUREAU-CABINET

PLATE 118

241. EARLY GEORGIAN PAINTED AND DECORATED SECRETAIRE
Courtesy of Biggs of Maidenhead Ltd.

PLATE 119

242. EARLY GEORGIAN DECORATED LACQUER SECRETAIRE
Victoria and Albert Museum Crown Copyright

PLATE 120

243. CHIPPENDALE CARVED MAHOGANY
UPHOLSTERED ARMCHAIR

244. CHIPPENDALE CARVED MAHOGANY
UPHOLSTERED ARMCHAIR

245. CHIPPENDALE CARVED MAHOGANY
UPHOLSTERED ARMCHAIR

246. CHIPPENDALE CARVED MAHOGANY
UPHOLSTERED ARMCHAIR

PLATE 121

247. CHIPPENDALE CARVED MAHOGANY SIDE CHAIR
Victoria and Albert Museum Crown Copyright

248. CHIPPENDALE CARVED MAHOGANY UPHOLSTERED ARMCHAIR
Courtesy of Needham's Antiques, Inc., New York City

249. CHIPPENDALE CARVED MAHOGANY UPHOLSTERED SIDE CHAIR WITH DOLPHIN FEET

250. CHIPPENDALE CARVED MAHOGANY ARMCHAIR
Sold at $1,200 a pair by Parke-Bernet Galleries, Inc., New York City

PLATE 122

251. CHIPPENDALE CARVED MAHOGANY UPHOLSTERED ARMCHAIR
Sold at $600 by Parke-Bernet Galleries, Inc., New York City

252. CHIPPENDALE CARVED MAHOGANY UPHOLSTERED ARMCHAIR
Sold at $1,000 by Parke-Bernet Galleries, Inc., New York City

253. CHIPPENDALE CARVED MAHOGANY UPHOLSTERED ARMCHAIR
Sold at $3,200 by Parke-Bernet Galleries, Inc., New York City

254. CHIPPENDALE CARVED MAHOGANY UPHOLSTERED ARMCHAIR
Sold at $1,800 by Parke-Bernet Galleries, Inc., New York City

PLATE 123

255. CHIPPENDALE CARVED MAHOGANY ARMCHAIR

256. CHIPPENDALE CARVED MAHOGANY RIBBON-BACK
ARMCHAIR
Victoria and Albert Museum Crown Copyright

257. CHIPPENDALE CARVED MAHOGANY RIBBON-BACK
SIDE CHAIR
Sold at $7,000 a pair by Parke-Bernet Galleries,
Inc., New York City

258. CHIPPENDALE CARVED MAHOGANY SIDE CHAIR
Courtesy of Needham's Antiques, Inc., New York City

PLATE 124

259. CHIPPENDALE CARVED MAHOGANY UPHOLSTERED SIDE CHAIR

260. CHIPPENDALE CARVED MAHOGANY UPHOLSTERED ARMCHAIR

261. CHIPPENDALE CARVED MAHOGANY UPHOLSTERED ARMCHAIR

262. CHIPPENDALE CARVED MAHOGANY UPHOLSTERED ARMCHAIR

PLATE 125

264. CHIPPENDALE CARVED WALNUT UPHOLSTERED ARMCHAIR

263. CHIPPENDALE CARVED MAHOGANY SIDE CHAIR

265. CHIPPENDALE CARVED MAHOGANY UPHOLSTERED SETTEE

PLATE 126

266. CHIPPENDALE CARVED MAHOGANY
SIDE CHAIR

267. CHIPPENDALE CARVED MAHOGANY
SIDE CHAIR

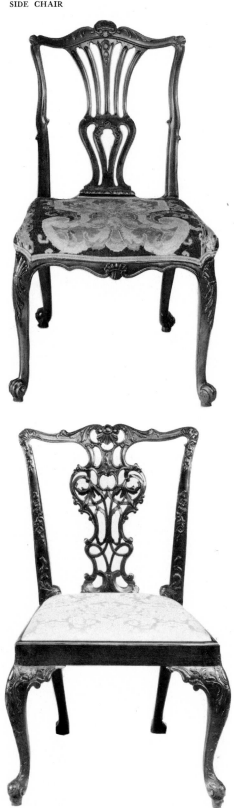

268. CHIPPENDALE CARVED MAHOGANY
SIDE CHAIR
Sold at $800 a pair by Parke-Bernet
Galleries, Inc., New York City

269. CHIPPENDALE CARVED MAHOGANY
SIDE CHAIR
Sold at $1,300 a pair by Parke-Bernet
Galleries, Inc., New York City

PLATE 127

270. CHIPPENDALE CARVED MAHOGANY TASSEL-BACK SETTEE

271. CHIPPENDALE CARVED MAHOGANY
ARMCHAIR
*Victoria and Albert Museum Crown
Copyright*

272. CHIPPENDALE CARVED MAHOGANY
ARMCHAIR
*Courtesy of French & Co., Inc., New York
City*

PLATE 128

273. CHIPPENDALE CARVED MAHOGANY
ARMCHAIR
*Courtesy of Needham's Antiques, Inc., New
York City*

274. CHIPPENDALE CARVED MAHOGANY
ARMCHAIR

275. CHIPPENDALE CARVED MAHOGANY SIDE
CHAIR

276. CHIPPENDALE CARVED MAHOGANY SIDE
CHAIR

PLATE 129

278. CHIPPENDALE CARVED MAHOGANY
ARMCHAIR
*Victoria and Albert Museum Crown
Copyright*

277. PHILADELPHIA CHIPPENDALE CARVED
MAHOGANY ARMCHAIR

279. CHIPPENDALE CARVED MAHOGANY THREE-CHAIR-BACK SETTEE
Sold at $1,000 by Parke-Bernet Galleries, Inc., New York City

PLATE 130

280. CHIPPENDALE CARVED MAHOGANY SIDE
CHAIR

281. AMERICAN CHIPPENDALE CARVED MAHOGANY
SIDE CHAIR

282. CHIPPENDALE CARVED MAHOGANY SIDE CHAIR
Victoria and Albert Museum Crown Copyright

283. CHIPPENDALE CARVED MAHOGANY ARMCHAIR
Sold at $560 a pair by Parke-Bernet
Galleries, Inc., New York City

PLATE 131

284. CHIPPENDALE CARVED MAHOGANY SIDE
CHAIR
From Bramshill Park, Hampshire

285. CHIPPENDALE CARVED MAHOGANY
ARMCHAIR
*Courtesy of J. J. Wolff (Antiques) Ltd., New
York City*

286. CHIPPENDALE CARVED MAHOGANY SIDE
CHAIR

287. CHIPPENDALE CARVED MAHOGANY SIDE
CHAIR
Sold at $3,450 for six by Parke-Bernet
Galleries, Inc., New York City

PLATE 132

288. CHIPPENDALE CARVED MAHOGANY
ARMCHAIR

289. CHIPPENDALE CARVED MAHOGANY SIDE
CHAIR

290. CHIPPENDALE CARVED MAHOGANY
ARMCHAIR

291. CHIPPENDALE CARVED MAHOGANY SIDE
CHAIR
Sold at $380 a pair by Parke-Bernet Galleries,
Inc., New York City

PLATE 133

292. CHIPPENDALE CARVED WALNUT RIBBON-AND-TASSEL BACK SIDE CHAIR
Courtesy of J. J. Wolff (Antiques) Ltd., New York City

293. CHIPPENDALE CARVED MAHOGANY SIDE CHAIR
Sold at $420 a pair by Parke-Bernet Galleries, Inc., New York City

294. CHIPPENDALE CARVED MAHOGANY SIDE CHAIR

295. CHIPPENDALE CARVED MAHOGANY ARM-CHAIR
Sold at $300 by Parke-Bernet Galleries, Inc., New York City

PLATE 134

296. CHIPPENDALE CARVED MAHOGANY SIDE
CHAIR
Courtesy of the Philadelphia Museum of Art

297. CHIPPENDALE CARVED MAHOGANY SIDE
CHAIR
Sold at $2,500 for ten by Parke-Bernet
Galleries, Inc., New York City

298. CHIPPENDALE CARVED MAHOGANY SIDE
CHAIR

299. CHIPPENDALE CARVED MAHOGANY SIDE
CHAIR
*Victoria and Albert Museum Crown
Copyright*

PLATE 135

300. CHIPPENDALE CARVED MAHOGANY SIDE CHAIR

301. CHIPPENDALE CARVED MAHOGANY SIDE CHAIR

302. CHIPPENDALE-HEPPLEWHITE CARVED MAHOGANY SIDE CHAIR

303. CHIPPENDALE CARVED MAHOGANY SIDE CHAIR

PLATE 136

304. CHIPPENDALE MAHOGANY LADDER-BACK
SIDE CHAIR

305. LATE GEORGIAN MAHOGANY LADDER-BACK
ARMCHAIR

306. CHIPPENDALE MAHOGANY LADDER-BACK
LIBRARY ARMCHAIR

307. CHIPPENDALE WALNUT STRADDLE CHAIR

PLATE 137

308. LATE CHIPPENDALE CARVED MAHOGANY
LADDER-BACK ARMCHAIR

309. CHIPPENDALE CARVED MAHOGANY
LADDER-BACK SIDE CHAIR
*Courtesy of Needham's Antiques, Inc., New
York City*

310. CHIPPENDALE CARVED MAHOGANY SIDE
CHAIR
*Courtesy of J. J. Wolff (Antiques) Ltd., New
York City*

311. LATE CHIPPENDALE CARVED MAHOGANY
LADDER-BACK SIDE CHAIR
*Victoria and Albert Museum Crown
Copyright*

PLATE 138

312. CHIPPENDALE CARVED MAHOGANY
ARMCHAIR

313. CHIPPENDALE CARVED MAHOGANY
RIBBON-BACK ARMCHAIR

314. CHIPPENDALE CARVED MAHOGANY SIDE
CHAIR
*Courtesy of J. J. Wolff (Antiques) Ltd., New
York City*

315. CHIPPENDALE CARVED MAHOGANY
ARMCHAIR
*Courtesy of the Kunstindustrimuseet, Oslo,
Norway*

PLATE 139

316. CHINESE CHIPPENDALE CARVED MAHOGANY ARMCHAIR
From Bramshill Park, Hampshire

PLATE 140

317. CHINESE CHIPPENDALE INLAID WALNUT
ARMCHAIR
*Victoria and Albert Museum Crown
Copyright*

318. CHINESE CHIPPENDALE CARVED MAHOGANY
ARMCHAIR

319. CHINESE CHIPPENDALE CARVED MAHOGANY
ARMCHAIR

320. CHINESE CHIPPENDALE CARVED MAHOGANY
SIDE CHAIR
Sold at $1,950 for six by Parke-Bernet
Galleries, Inc., New York City

PLATE 141

321. CHINESE CHIPPENDALE CARVED MAHOGANY
SIDE CHAIR
Sold at $1,400 for four by Parke-Bernet
Galleries, Inc., New York City

322. CHINESE CHIPPENDALE CARVED MAHOGANY
ARMCHAIR

PLATE 142

323. CHINESE CHIPPENDALE CARVED MAHOGANY TWO-CHAIR-BACK SETTEE
Courtesy of Colonial Williamsburg, Williamsburg, Virginia

PLATE 143

PLATE 144

325. CHIPPENDALE CARVED MAHOGANY
UPHOLSTERED OPEN-ARM EASY CHAIR
Courtesy of J. J. Wolff (Antiques) Ltd.,
New York City

326. CHIPPENDALE FRET-CARVED MAHOGANY STOOL
Courtesy of J. J. Wolff (Antiques) Ltd., New York
City

327–328. PAIR OF CHIPPENDALE CARVED MAHOGANY UPHOLSTERED OPEN-ARM EASY CHAIRS
Sold at $4,000 by Parke-Bernet Galleries, Inc., New York City

PLATE 145

329. CHIPPENDALE CARVED MAHOGANY UPHOLSTERED OPEN-ARM EASY CHAIR
Sold at $8,000 by Parke-Bernet Galleries, Inc., New York City

PLATE 146

330–331. PAIR OF CHIPPENDALE CARVED MAHOGANY UPHOLSTERED OPEN-ARM EASY CHAIRS

332. CHIPPENDALE FRET-CARVED CHERRY
UPHOLSTERED OPEN-ARM EASY CHAIR
Sold at $800 a pair by Parke-Bernet Galleries,
Inc., New York City

333. LATE CHIPPENDALE CARVED MAHOGANY
UPHOLSTERED OPEN-ARM EASY CHAIR
Sold at $1,000 a pair by Parke-Bernet Galleries,
Inc., New York City

PLATE 147

334. CHIPPENDALE CARVED MAHOGANY
TRIPOD WINE STAND

335. CHIPPENDALE CARVED MAHOGANY
TRIPOD WINE STAND
*Victoria and Albert Museum Crown
Copyright*

336. CHIPPENDALE CARVED MAHOGANY
TORCHÈRE
Sold at $2,100 a pair by Parke-Bernet
Galleries, Inc., New York City

337. CHIPPENDALE CARVED MAHOGANY
TORCHÈRE

PLATE 148

339. CHIPPENDALE CARVED MAHOGANY BASIN
STAND
Sold at $425 by Parke-Bernet Galleries, Inc.,
New York Cty

340. CHIPPENDALE CARVED MAHOGANY CHEVAL SCREEN
WITH CHINESE PAINTED PAPER PANEL

338. CHIPPENDALE CARVED MAHOGANY BASIN
STAND
Sold at $1,300 by Parke-Bernet Galleries,
Inc., New York City

PLATE 149

343. CHIPPENDALE MAHOGANY TRIPOD
POLE SCREEN WITH NEEDLEWORK PANEL

342. CHIPPENDALE CARVED MAHOGANY
TRIPOD POLE SCREEN WITH NEEDLE-
WORK PANEL

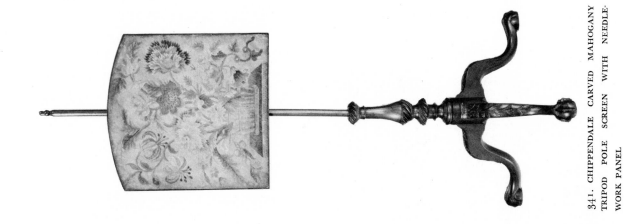

341. CHIPPENDALE CARVED MAHOGANY
TRIPOD POLE SCREEN WITH NEEDLE-
WORK PANEL

PLATE 150

345. CHIPPENDALE CARVED MAHOGANY TRIPOD
FIRE SCREEN WITH NEEDLEWORK PANEL
Courtesy of Needham's Antiques, Inc.,
New York City

346. CHIPPENDALE CARVED MAHOGANY TRIPOD TABLE
Sold at $2,650 by Parke-Bernet Galleries, Inc., New
York City

344. CHIPPENDALE CARVED MAHOGANY
TRIPOD POLE SCREEN WITH TAPESTRY
PANEL

PLATE 151

349. CHIPPENDALE CARVED MAHOGANY
TRIPOD TABLE
Sold at $3,700 by Parke-Bernet Galleries,
Inc., New York City

348. CHIPPENDALE CARVED MAHOGANY TRIPOD TABLE

347. CHIPPENDALE CARVED MAHOGANY TRIPOD TABLE
Sold at $2,800 by Parke-Bernet Galleries, Inc., New York City

PLATE 152

350. CHIPPENDALE CARVED TRIPOD TABLE
Victoria and Albert Museum Crown Copyright

PLATE 153

351. CHIPPENDALE CARVED MAHOGANY LOW TRIPOD TABLE

352. CHIPPENDALE CARVED MAHOGANY LOW TRIPOD TABLE

353. CHIPPENDALE CARVED MAHOGANY LOW TRIPOD TABLE

354. CHIPPENDALE CARVED MAHOGANY TRIPOD STAND WITH FRET GALLERY
Sold at $900 by Parke-Bernet Galleries, Inc., New York City

PLATE 154

355. CHIPPENDALE CARVED MAHOGANY TRIPOD
TABLE WITH SPINDLE GALLERY
Sold at $1,500 by Parke-Bernet Galleries,
Inc., New York City

356. CHIPPENDALE CARVED MAHOGANY TRIPOD
TABLE WITH SPINDLE GALLERY
Sold at $1,500 by Parke-Bernet Galleries,
Inc., New York City

PLATE 155

357. CHIPPENDALE CARVED MAHOGANY TRIPOD
TABLE WITH FRET-PIERCED GALLERY
Sold at £682 by Christie, Manson & Woods,
London

358. CHIPPENDALE CARVED MAHOGANY TRIPOD
TABLE
Sold at £336 by Christie, Manson & Woods,
London

PLATE 156

359. CHIPPENDALE CARVED MAHOGANY TRIPOD
TABLE
Sold at $600 by Parke-Bernet Galleries, Inc.,
New York City

360. CHIPPENDALE CARVED MAHOGANY TABLE

361. CHIPPENDALE CARVED MAHOGANY TRIPOD
TABLE
Sold at $500 by Parke-Bernet Galleries, Inc.,
New York City

362. CHIPPENDALE CARVED MAHOGANY TRIPOD
TABLE
Sold at $675 by Parke-Bernet Galleries, Inc.,
New York City

PLATE 157

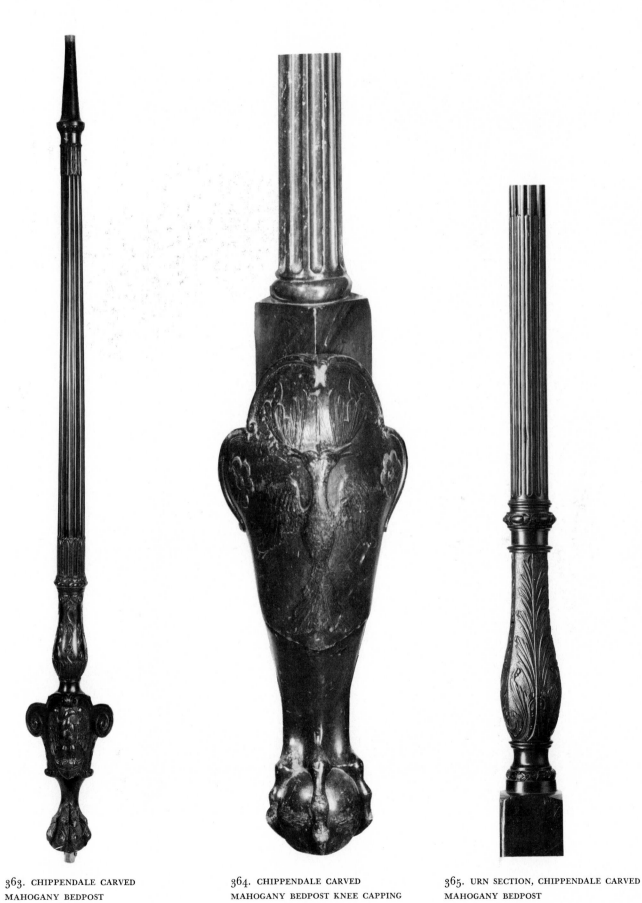

363. CHIPPENDALE CARVED
MAHOGANY BEDPOST

364. CHIPPENDALE CARVED
MAHOGANY BEDPOST KNEE CAPPING

365. URN SECTION, CHIPPENDALE CARVED
MAHOGANY BEDPOST

PLATE 158

366. CHIPPENDALE CARVED AND PARCEL-GILDED MAHOGANY BEDSTEAD

PLATE 159

367. CHIPPENDALE DECORATED BLACK AND GOLD LACQUER BEDSTEAD FROM BADMINTON HOUSE, GLOUCESTERSHIRE
Victoria and Albert Museum Crown Copyright

PLATE 160

369. CHIPPENDALE INLAID AND FRET-CARVED MAHOGANY URN STAND

368. CHIPPENDALE CARVED MAHOGANY URN STAND
Sold at $625 by Parke-Bernet Galleries, Inc., New York City

370. CHIPPENDALE FRET-CARVED MAHOGANY URN STAND

372. CHIPPENDALE LABURNUM PARQUETRY COFFRET ON STAND WITH SILVER MOUNTS
Courtesy of Hotspur Ltd., London

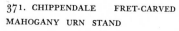

371. CHIPPENDALE FRET-CARVED MAHOGANY URN STAND

PLATE 161

373. CHIPPENDALE CARVED MAHOGANY
SILVER TABLE WITH FRET GALLERY
*Victoria and Albert Museum Crown
Copyright*

374. CHIPPENDALE MAHOGANY TRAY-
TOP SILVER TABLE
Sold at $750 by Parke-Bernet
Galleries, Inc., New York City

PLATE 162

375. CHIPPENDALE MAHOGANY
SILVER TABLE

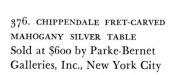

376. CHIPPENDALE FRET-CARVED
MAHOGANY SILVER TABLE
Sold at $600 by Parke-Bernet
Galleries, Inc., New York City

PLATE 163

377. CHIPPENDALE CARVED
MAHOGANY SILVER TABLE

378. CHIPPENDALE FRET-CARVED
MAHOGANY SILVER TABLE
Sold at $775 by Parke-Bernet
Galleries, Inc., New York City

PLATE 164

379. CHIPPENDALE FRET-CARVED
MAHOGANY SILVER TABLE
Sold at $900 by Parke-Bernet
Galleries, Inc., New York City

380. CHIPPENDALE CARVED
MAHOGANY SILVER TABLE

PLATE 165

381. GEORGIAN MAHOGANY SPIDER-
LEG TABLE WITH SPINDLE GALLERY

382. GEORGIAN INLAID MAHOGANY
SPIDER-LEG DROP-LEAF TABLE

PLATE 166

383. CHIPPENDALE MAHOGANY AND
PLUM PUDDING MAHOGANY
DROP-LEAF TABLE
Sold at $450 by Parke-Bernet
Galleries, Inc., New York City

384. CHIPPENDALE MAHOGANY
DROP-LEAF TABLE

PLATE 167

385. CHIPPENDALE INLAID LABURNUM
WOOD DROP-LEAF TABLE
*Courtesy of Mallett & Son
(Antiques) Ltd., London*

386. CHIPPENDALE MAHOGANY
DROP-LEAF TABLE
*Courtesy of J. J. Wolff (Antiques)
Ltd., New York City*

PLATE 168

387. CHIPPENDALE CARVED
MAHOGANY DROP-LEAF TABLE

388. CHIPPENDALE MAHOGANY
TRIANGULAR DROP-LEAF TABLE

PLATE 169

389. CHIPPENDALE CARVED MAHOGANY WRITING TABLE

PLATE 170

390. CHIPPENDALE FRET-CARVED
MAHOGANY ARCHITECT'S TABLE
*Victoria and Albert Museum
Crown Copyright*

391. CHIPPENDALE MAHOGANY WRITING TABLE

PLATE 171

392. CHIPPENDALE MAHOGANY WRITING TABLE

393. CHIPPENDALE CARVED MAHOGANY WRITING TABLE
Sold at $700 by Parke-Bernet Galleries, Inc., New York City

PLATE 172

394. CHIPPENDALE CARVED
MAHOGANY SIDE TABLE

395. CHIPPENDALE CARVED MAHOGANY
KNEEHOLE WRITING DESK
Sold at $1,300 by Parke-Bernet
Galleries, Inc., New York City

PLATE 173

396. CHIPPENDALE CARVED MAHOGANY PARTNER'S DESK
Sold at $5,000 by Parke-Bernet Galleries, Inc., New York City

PLATE 174

398. CHIPPENDALE MAHOGANY PEDESTAL DESK
Sold at $1,300 by Parke-Bernet Galleries, Inc., New York City

397. CHIPPENDALE MAHOGANY KNEEHOLE WRITING DESK
Sold at $1,100 by Parke-Bernet Galleries, Inc., New York City

PLATE 175

399. CHIPPENDALE INLAID MAHOGANY PEDESTAL DESK
Courtesy of Mallett & Son (Antiques) Ltd., London

PLATE 176

400. CHIPPENDALE CARVED MAHOGANY
CARD TABLE
Sold at $2,500 a pair by Parke-Bernet
Galleries, Inc., New York City

401. CHIPPENDALE CARVED MAHOGANY
CARD TABLE

PLATE 177

402. CHIPPENDALE CARVED MAHOGANY
CARD TABLE

403. CHIPPENDALE CARVED MAHOGANY
CARD TABLE
Sold at $1,050 by Parke-Bernet
Galleries, Inc., New York City

PLATE 178

404. CHIPPENDALE CARVED
MAHOGANY CARD TABLE

405. CHIPPENDALE CARVED
MAHOGANY CARD TABLE
*Courtesy of J. J. Wolff (Antiques)
Ltd., New York City*

PLATE 179

406. CHIPPENDALE CARVED MAHOGANY
SERPENTINE CARD TABLE

407. LATE CHIPPENDALE CARVED
MAHOGANY CARD TABLE

PLATE 180

408. CHIPPENDALE CARVED MAHOGANY
CONSOLE
*Courtesy of J. J. Wolff (Antiques)
Ltd., New York City*

409. CHIPPENDALE CARVED AND GILDED
CONSOLE

PLATE 181

410. CHIPPENDALE CARVED MAHOGANY SIDE TABLE
Victoria and Albert Museum Crown Copyright

411. CHIPPENDALE CARVED
MAHOGANY SIDE TABLE

PLATE 182

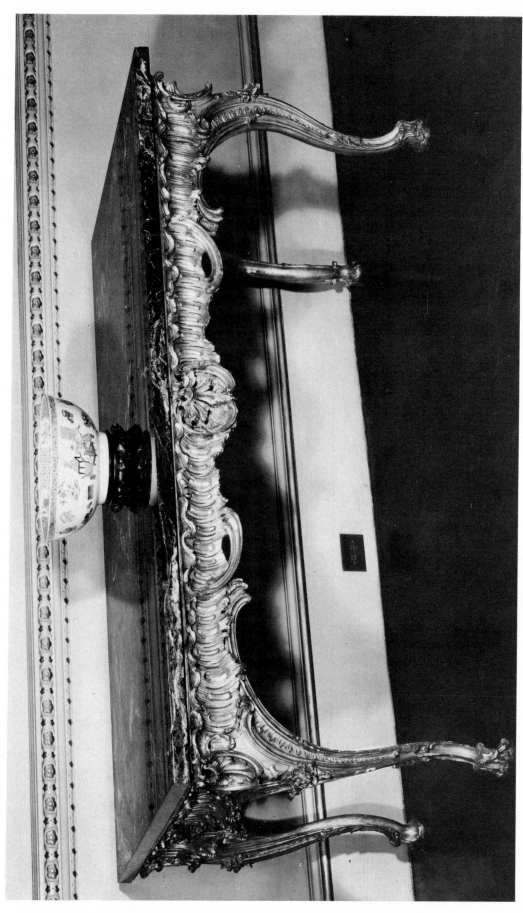

412. CHIPPENDALE CARVED AND GILDED SIDE TABLE
Sold at $1,400 by Parke-Bernet Galleries, Inc., New York City

PLATE 183

413. CHIPPENDALE CARVED MAHOGANY SIDE TABLE
Courtesy of J. J. Wolff (Antiques) Ltd., New York City

PLATE 184

414. CHIPPENDALE CARVED MAHOGANY WRITING AND DRESSING TABLE
Sold at $1,000 by Parke-Bernet Galleries, Inc., New York City

415. CHIPPENDALE CARVED MAHOGANY SIDE TABLE

PLATE 185

416. CHIPPENDALE CARVED MAHOGANY SIDE TABLE

PLATE 186

417. CHIPPENDALE CARVED MAHOGANY SIDE TABLE

418. CHIPPENDALE CARVED MAHOGANY
AND WALNUT SIDE TABLE

PLATE 187

419. CHIPPENDALE CARVED MAHOGANY SIDE TABLE
Victoria and Albert Museum Crown Copyright

PLATE 188

420. CHIPPENDALE DECORATED LACQUER COMMODE-CABINET FROM BADMINTON HOUSE, GLOUCESTERSHIRE

Victoria and Albert Museum Crown Copyright

PLATE 189

421. INTERIOR VIEW, KILKEA,
as shown in the
Irish Tatler & Sketch

PLATE 190

422. CHIPPENDALE CARVED
MAHOGANY ARCHITECTURAL
COMMODE

423. CHIPPENDALE CARVED
MAHOGANY ARCHITECTURAL
COMMODE

PLATE 191

424. CHIPPENDALE CARVED MAHOGANY KNEEHOLE LIBRARY TABLE COLLECTION OF THE MARQUESS OF LINCOLNSHIRE
Sold at $3,000 by Parke-Bernet Galleries, Inc., New York City

PLATE 192

425. CHIPPENDALE CARVED MAHOGANY COMMODE
Victoria and Albert Museum
Crown Copyright

426. CHIPPENDALE CARVED WALNUT COMMODE
Sold at $3,250 by Parke-Bernet Galleries, Inc., New York City

PLATE 193

427. CHIPPENDALE CARVED MAHOGANY COMMODE-SECRETAIRE
Courtesy of G. Jetley, Ltd., London

PLATE 194

428. CHINESE CHIPPENDALE CARVED
MAHOGANY KNEEHOLE COMMODE
Sold at $3,500 by Parke-Bernet
Galleries, Inc., New York City

429. CHIPPENDALE FRET-CARVED
MAHOGANY KNEEHOLE DRESSING TABLE

PLATE 195

430. CHIPPENDALE CARVED MAHOGANY COMMODE
Sold at $5,900 by Parke-Bernet Galleries, Inc., New York City

PLATE 196

431. CHIPPENDALE MAHOGANY COMMODE
Courtesy of Biggs of Maidenhead Ltd.

432. CHIPPENDALE MAHOGANY COMMODE

PLATE 197

433. CHIPPENDALE MAHOGANY SECRETAIRE
WITH OPEN-FRETTED SHELVES

PLATE 198

434. CHIPPENDALE FRET-CARVED MAHOGANY
CHEST-ON-CHEST
*Courtesy of the Philadelphia Museum of
Art*

435. CHIPPENDALE FRET-CARVED MAHOGANY
CHEST-ON-CHEST

PLATE 199

436. CHIPPENDALE CARVED MAHOGANY BUREAU
Courtesy of J. J. Wolff (Antiques) Ltd., New York City

437. CHIPPENDALE MAHOGANY BUREAU
Courtesy of Needham's Antiques, Inc., New York City

PLATE 200

438. CHIPPENDALE MAHOGANY BUREAU

439. CHIPPENDALE MAHOGANY BUREAU

PLATE 201

440. CHIPPENDALE CARVED MAHOGANY
KETTLE-BASE SECRETAIRE

PLATE 202

441. CHIPPENDALE FRET-CARVED MAHOGANY SECRETAIRE
Sold at $3,500 by Parke-Bernet Galleries, Inc., New York City

PLATE 203

442. CHIPPENDALE CARVED MAHOGANY SECRETAIRE
Courtesy of Temple Williams, Ltd., London

PLATE 204

443. CHIPPENDALE CARVED MAHOGANY SECRETAIRE

PLATE 205

444. CHIPPENDALE CARVED MAHOGANY SECRETAIRE

PLATE 206

445. CHIPPENDALE FRET-CARVED MAHOGANY SECRETAIRE

PLATE 207

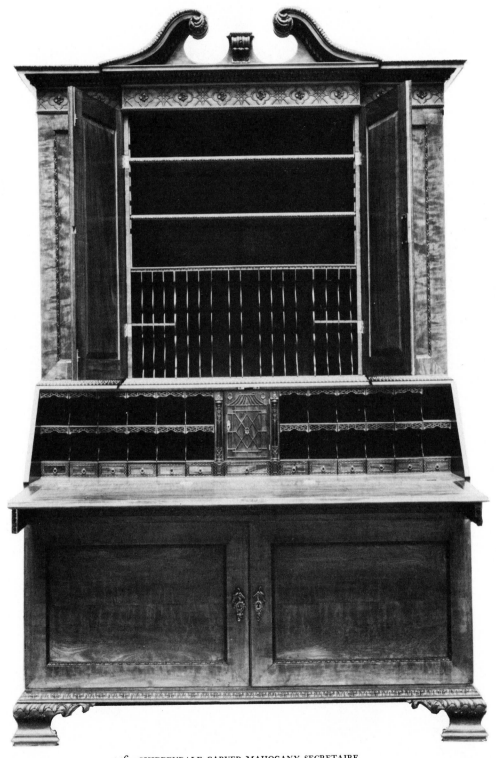

446. CHIPPENDALE CARVED MAHOGANY SECRETAIRE
Victoria and Albert Museum Crown Copyright

PLATE 208

447. CHINESE CHIPPENDALE CARVED MAHOGANY BUREAU-CABINET

PLATE 209

448. CHINESE CHIPPENDALE CARVED MAHOGANY BUREAU-CABINET

PLATE 210

449. CHIPPENDALE CARVED
MAHOGANY TEA CADDY

450. CHIPPENDALE CARVED
MAHOGANY HANGING SHELVES

PLATE 211

452. CHIPPENDALE FRET-CARVED MAHOGANY HANGING SHELVES
Sold at $950 a pair by Parke-Bernet Galleries, Inc., New York City

451. CHIPPENDALE MAHOGANY OPEN-FRET HANGING SHELVES
Courtesy of J. J. Wolff (Antiques) Ltd., New York City

PLATE 212

453. CHIPPENDALE FRET-CARVED MAHOGANY DISPLAY CABINET
Sold at $1,100 by Parke-Bernet Galleries, Inc., New York City

PLATE 213

454. CHINESE CHIPPENDALE CARVED MAHOGANY DISPLAY CABINET
Courtesy of the Royal Ontario Museum, Toronto

PLATE 214

455. CHIPPENDALE CARVED AND PARCEL-GILDED PADAUK WRITING CABINET

PLATE 215

456. CHIPPENDALE CARVED
AND PARCEL-GILDED
WALNUT CABINET

PLATE 216

457. CHIPPENDALE CARVED MAHOGANY WARDROBE

PLATE 217

458. CHIPPENDALE CARVED MAHOGANY WARDROBE

PLATE 218

459. CHIPPENDALE FRET-CARVED AND PAINTED CORNER CABINET

PLATE 219

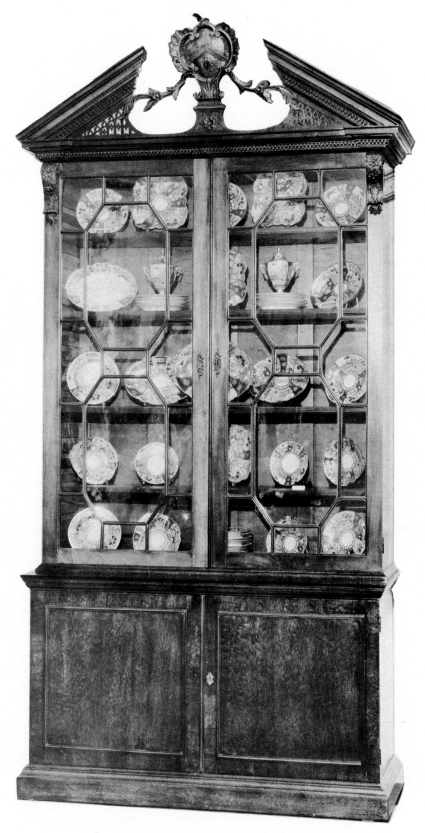

460. CHIPPENDALE CARVED MAHOGANY PIER CABINET

PLATE 220

461. CHIPPENDALE CARVED MAHOGANY BREAKFRONT BOOKCASE

PLATE 221

462. CHIPPENDALE MAHOGANY BREAKFRONT BOOKCASE
Courtesy of J. J. Wolff (Antiques) Ltd., New York City

PLATE 222

463. CHIPPENDALE MAHOGANY BREAKFRONT BOOKCASE

PLATE 223

464. CHIPPENDALE MAHOGANY BREAKFRONT BOOKCASE

PLATE 224

465. GEORGIAN "GUILT LEATHER AND PAINTED SCREEN"

PLATE 225

466. CHINESE PAINTED PAPER PANELS IN AN EIGHTEENTH-CENTURY SETTING

INDEX

Italic figures refer to illustrations.